Individual Rights and Civic Responsibility

THE RIGHT TO VOTE

Claudia Isler

The Rosen Publishing Group, Inc.
New York

Published in 2001 by The Rosen Publishing Group, Inc.
29 East 21st Street, New York, NY 10010

First Edition

Cover image: The Constitution of the United States of America

Library of Congress Cataloging-in-Publication Data

Isler, Claudia.
    The right to vote / by Claudia Isler. — 1st ed.
    p. cm. — (Individual rights, civic responsibility)
Includes bibliographical references and index.
ISBN 0-8239-3235-4 (library binding)
1. Suffrage—United States—History—Juvenile literature.
[1. Suffrage—History.] I. Title. II. Series.
JK1846 .I75 2000
324.6'2'0973—dc21
                                                    00-010495

Manufactured in the United States of America

About the Author

Claudia Isler is a freelance editor and writer who has edited material ranging in subject matter from robotic engineering to soap operas. She has written other Rosen books for young people, including *Caught in the Middle: A Teen Guide to Custody*, and two books about service-learning. She lives in Pennsylvania with her husband and their cat, Phoebe.

For my brothers, Adam, Eric, and Joshua, who taught me (the hard way) to fight for my rights, and for my parents, Stephanie Stern and Alan Isler, for teaching me that everyone's rights are the same.

Contents

1 You and Your Right to Vote

To understand why it's important to stay informed about issues that affect the world, your country, your state, or the city where you live, you need to know some simple facts. How does government work? If a law is unfair, how do we change it? Why do we vote? Is voting really that important?

A lot of people take their right to vote for granted. They watch the news or read the paper and complain about what the mayor of New York did last week, what the president of the United States did last year, or what they're teaching kids in school these days. Some people plan to vote for someone else, a new mayor or president, at the next election. But some of those people who are unhappy with the way things are going won't vote at all. They don't understand that voting is a way to make their voices heard. They let the people who do vote make the decisions for them. And they don't remember all the people who fought so hard, at so much personal sacrifice, to win the right to vote.

The Basics

Let's start with the basics. In a way, your government is made up of many governments. The federal government, whose offices are in Washington, DC, shares its power with the governments of each state, and each state with the governments of each city and town. Congress, a part of the federal government, is made up of the Senate and the House of Representatives. Congress creates laws. The president, vice president, and the Supreme Court are also part of the federal government. The president represents the executive branch of the federal government. This is the branch that enforces laws. The Supreme Court makes sure all the laws passed by Congress are fair.

Why are there so many government offices and departments? When the writers of the U.S. Constitution were working out a plan for government, they wanted to make sure that the central government would not have so much power that the people's rights would be limited. They wanted to create a system in which none of the branches of government would have too much power, so they created a system of "checks and balances." Each branch of the government has the power to undo what the other branches do. For example, the president can veto (reject) laws passed by Congress, Congress can override (dismiss) the president's veto, and the Supreme Court and other federal courts can overturn laws that violate (go against) the Constitution. The president picks the members of the Supreme Court. Congress can make changes to the Constitution with approval from three-quarters of the states.

7

The Bill of Rights

Amendment I

...ting an establishment of religion, or prohibiting the free exerci... ...f the people peaceably to assemble, and to petition the Govern...

Amendment II

...ary to the security of a free State, the right of the people to kee...

Amendment III

...e quartered in any house, without the consent of the Owner, n...

Amendment IV

...in their persons, houses, papers, and effects, against unreasona... ...ut upon probable cause, supported by Oath or affirmation, a... ...o be seized.

Amendment V

...r a capital, or otherwise infamous crime, unless on a presen... ...al forces, or in the Militia, when in actual service in time of... ...to be twice put in jeopardy of life or limb; nor shall be co... ...of life, liberty, or property, without due process of law; nor...

Amendment VI

...d shall enjoy the right to a speedy and public trial, by an i... ...itted, which district shall have been previously ascertained... ...confronted with the witnesses against him; to have compulsor... ...ounsel for his defence.

Amendment VII

...se in controversy shall exceed twenty dollars, the right of tri... ...amined in any Court of the United States, than according to...

Amendment VIII

...excessive fines imposed, nor cruel and unu...

The Bill of Rights guarantees American citizens many freedoms, such as the right to vote.

The Constitution

The Constitution, which defines the structure and power of the federal government, was written in 1787. It was ratified (approved) by eleven of the thirteen states in 1789. A change to the Constitution is called an amendment. The first ten amendments to the U.S. Constitution are called the Bill of Rights. The Bill of Rights was adopted in 1791. The Bill of Rights guarantees American citizens many freedoms that we take for granted, such as the freedom to practice one's religion, freedom to openly and publicly criticize the government, and the freedom to gather in protest. It also offers the guarantee of a military to protect us, a lawyer to defend us if we go to trial, and an impartial jury at that trial. The Bill of Rights is supposed to protect us from being searched by force without authorization, from having our property taken without our permission, and from being cruelly punished for any crime we may commit or be suspected of committing. Some of the other rights guaranteed in the first ten amendments refer to experiences from the American Revolution: "No soldier shall, in time of peace, be quartered in [live in] any house, without the consent of the owner, nor in time of war, but in a manner to be prescribed by law." When this was written, people could remember quite clearly the British troops who had taken over their homes and eaten all their food.

Changing the Constitution

There have been many times that different groups have wanted changes (amendments) made to the Constitution. In this book, there are three groups in particular whose

9

struggles to make changes will be of interest to us: African Americans, women, and young people. These groups of people wanted to make changes that would give them rights as full citizens of the United States. They wanted the right to vote.

How to Make an Amendment

Changing the Constitution is not easy. Changes are serious business. Let's say you want to add a new right to the Constitution. You want to make it law that Thursdays will be all-the-ice-cream-you-can-eat-for-one–dollar days all over the country, in every state, city, and town. The first thing you'll need to do is find others to support your cause, because it is very unlikely that you'll be able to convince Congress all by yourself. Who ever heard of government-regulated ice cream days? Once you've got your group of supporters together, you'll want to get other groups involved who might share your passion for the cause, like the Dairy Farmer Association or companies that produce ice cream. Now that you have all those people to work for the cause, you need to prepare the amendment you hope to get passed.

> *Section 1. The right of the citizens of the United States to have all the ice cream they can eat on Thursday of every week for the price of one dollar shall not be denied or abridged by the United States or by any State on account of national or state holidays. Section 2. The Congress shall have the power to enforce this article by appropriate legislation.*

Make copies of your amendment proposal and get it published in every newspaper and magazine in the country. Talk about your amendment on television shows, get as much support from the American people as you can, and most importantly, make sure that a copy of the amendment finds its way onto the desk of every senator, congressman, and congresswoman in Washington. Wasn't that simple?

How to Pass an Amendment

Now you've gotten the attention of a lot of people in the government. You and your fellow ice cream fans are speaking at ice cream rallies where members of the American Medical Association are interrupting your speeches with shouts about eating healthy and avoiding heart disease. Manufacturers of ice cream accessories are pelting you with sugar cones, waffle cones, and sprinkles. They don't like your amendment because they believe it will cost them too much money and put them out of business. Religious groups that believe eating dessert is a sin are publishing articles all over the country that say you and your followers are evil and will eventually destroy the society we live in. Despite the difficulties, you travel all over the country, trying to get Americans to agree with your point of view. They think you're the strangest person they've ever met, but some of them like what you have to say. They start talking to their friends about you. They start writing to their representatives in Congress to say that ice cream Thursdays should be a right of every American.

The Right to Vote

Years go by before you can find a single congressional representative willing to propose your resolution (a law that has not yet been passed). The day arrives, and she stands up in Congress to read it. The laughter is so loud, no can hear the one other congressman who says he supports the resolution. It does not go to a vote. Year after year, you work to convince your representative to reintroduce your resolution, all the while trying to convince other representatives to support it. Ten years pass, and your doctor has told you that you may not have any more ice cream. You decide to keep up the fight on behalf of those who will enjoy ice cream in the future. Your cause has been getting an increasing amount of support in Congress, but when it is debated again, a number of senators point out that it is not important enough to change the Constitution. Leave it up to each state, they say.

You get the idea. It is just not easy to change the way people think or do things, and that is what changing the Constitution is all about. When the Constitution outlawed slavery, it demanded that many Americans who had always had slaves suddenly accept that it was wrong to have slaves. Those Americans who had always believed that white people had more rights than black people were told to change their way of thinking. Later, when women began to demand their rights, including the right to vote, many people, including some women, had a hard time understanding that women had the right and the ability to be more than wives, mothers, pretty playthings, and unpaid workers. As you read on, you will see how difficult it is to make changes of this kind. People can be slow to change, especially if you're asking them to change what they believe is true.

Voting for Change

On the other hand, people and laws do change. The Constitution over the years has accumulated twenty-seven amendments. And this is where voting comes in. It is important to remember that when you choose someone to vote for, you are choosing someone who will represent you in the government. That means that you need to choose someone whose views and beliefs about certain issues and ideas agree with yours. And you have to consider the power that elected officials will have, and how that will affect your life. Take, for example, the president. The president gets to choose the members, or justices, that will sit on the Supreme Court. The Supreme Court makes very big decisions. It was the Supreme Court that made it illegal to keep black children from attending the same schools as white children by declaring that separate was not equal. It was the Supreme Court that gave women the right to have an abortion, and it is the Supreme Court that may take that right away. Your job is to elect a president who will appoint justices likely to make decisions you approve of. If the government that represents you right now is making one decision after another that makes you angry or goes against what you believe, you have the power to change that situation. Your power comes from your right to free speech and your right to peaceful protest, and from your ability to vote.

Who Doesn't Vote?

In the 1996 presidential election, less than half of the men and women eligible to do so cast their vote for a candidate.

13

Only 48 percent of all male citizens aged eighteen or above went to the polls to choose their president. Forty-nine percent of female citizens voted, putting them only slightly ahead of the men. Only 35 percent of eligible people identifying themselves as African American voted. Only 33 percent of voters between the ages of eighteen and twenty-nine voted. Even within the group with the largest turnout, people aged fifty to sixty-four, only 58 percent came to the polls to vote.

How to Vote

There are some requirements you must meet in order to vote. You must be at least eighteen years old, you must be an American citizen, you must register to vote, and you have to show proof of where you live to register. Usually, registering to vote just means filling out a simple form. It is free, and you don't need to be a member of a political party to register. Usually, you can find voter registration forms at the post office, at school, and often in the mall, if a neighborhood group is having a voter registration drive. If you can't find any forms, you can call your city board of elections or town hall to find out where you can register. In some places, you can even fill the form out on the Internet!

Some time after you register, you will receive a voter registration card in the mail, which you should sign. It usually tells you what election district you live in and where you should go to vote. Often, voting booths can be found in school cafeterias or gyms at election time, so you've probably seen them! Different places use different methods to record your votes. In some places, you step into a private booth and pull a lever to close a curtain behind you. Then

A young woman is in a voting booth, getting ready to exercise her constitutional right to vote.

you simply flip a switch next to the name of the person you're voting for until an 'X' appears in the box closest to the name. In other places, you don't close yourself into a booth, but you still have privacy. The person in charge, called a registrar, will give you a card that has on it the names of the people who are running for office. At your table, you punch a hole in the card next to the name of the person you are voting for. It is a simple thing to do.

The amazing thing is that so many people never bother to take advantage of this system. Your power to vote comes from the hard work and dedication of a lot of people who believed in you before you were ever born. They believed that you would be born with the ability and the intelligence to think for yourself and choose your leaders. They made sure you would be born with the right to vote.

2 African Americans and the Right to Vote

Amendment XV

Section 1. *The right of citizens of the United States to vote shall not be denied or abridged by the United States or by any State on account of race, color, or previous condition of servitude.*

Section 2. *The Congress shall have power to enforce this article by appropriate legislation.*

The story of the struggle for African American voting rights is not a simple one. It has its roots in slavery. It is impossible to talk about black suffrage (voting rights) without looking at the effects of slavery, the period known as Reconstruction, and the daily battle African Americans had to fight for the most basic human rights. Even after the passage of the Thirteenth, Fourteenth, and Fifteenth Amendments to the United States Constitution, blacks were not free to take advantage of all that democracy offered. They were not allowed to participate. As you read on, you'll find that there were different forces at work to keep blacks from advancing economically or socially, and that it was not always kindness or high moral standards that fueled the effort to give them their rights.

A Brief History of Slavery

During the first forty years after the establishment of the Virginia colony, blacks owned land, voted, and held public office. This was true in other colonies too. New York granted freedom to indentured Africans in 1644. An indentured servant was one who signed a contract to work for a certain number of years. Slavery began as a temporary state, and having a christening or baptism could win a slave his or her freedom. But by 1682, Virginia had passed a law that made slavery a lifelong condition. By the time of the American Revolution, there were 500,000 slaves in the colonies, an increase of 450,000 from just sixty years earlier.

The ideas that started the American Revolution—independence, freedom, and human rights—had some effect on slavery. A few colonies passed measures against the slave trade and some people freed their slaves. Abolition (anti-slavery) societies began to organize and worked to educate those blacks who had been freed. One by one, however, the states took away blacks' right to vote. By the time of the Civil War in 1861, blacks could not vote in any state except five of the New England states, and there was not a large enough African-American population there to make a difference. By the late 1850s, there were nearly four million

17

black slaves in the United Sates, and "slave codes" were enacted to keep those slaves uneducated and defenseless. They were not allowed to gather in groups of more than five. They needed a pass to leave the plantations where they lived and worked. Any religious meetings they held had to have white supervision, and it was actually against the law to teach a black person to read and write.

This kind of prejudice, which was certainly the rule in the South but common enough in the North as well, made it possible for the government to pass federal laws and make legal judgments that hurt African Americans. One example is the 1850 Fugitive Slave Act, which required state and local governments to help capture runaway slaves and return them to their owners. Another is the Supreme Court's decision in the *Dred Scott* case of 1857. Slaves and their descendants were found to be property, not citizens of the United States.

The conflict between slavery and antislavery groups helped set off the Civil War. Southern states seceded, or removed themselves, from the Union, and tried to form their own country, called the Confederacy. In 1863, President Abraham Lincoln's Emancipation Proclamation freed all slaves in the states or parts of states that were still fighting against the Union. This meant huge changes for the South. In South Carolina, Mississippi, and Louisiana, blacks made up the majority of the population. In Virginia and North Carolina, they made up 40 percent of the total population.

Reconstruction

Following the Civil War between the Northern and Southern states (1861–1865) there was a period known as

In 1863, President Lincoln's Emancipation Proclamation freed all slaves in the states or parts of states that were still fighting against the Union.

Reconstruction, which lasted until 1877. Reconstruction was a time of reorganization, growth, and great progress in the United States. The South had much to recover from. The war had left its buildings and homes burned, armies had ruined the countryside, and farmlands were ruined because of poor or no cultivation. People were starving and suffering from disease. Political forces were at work to change the way the South made its money. The North worked to end slave-based plantation profits.

The South now had a huge population of newly free blacks, who would expect to work for pay and might, people feared, seek some revenge for years of suffering at the hands of white masters. Former slaves had no homes, no jobs, and simply wandered. Ex-Confederates were nervous, and looked for ways to hold on to the power they'd had for so long. The Thirteenth Amendment, passed in

19

1865, abolished slavery. The movement of African Americans from slavery into freedom made enormous changes in the country that eventually led to the passage of the Fourteenth Amendment, which defined who was a citizen, and what citizens' rights were. The Fifteenth Amendment to the Constitution gave African American men the vote. The war-torn South had to rebuild its economy based on free labor instead of slave labor.

Restoring seceded states to their places in the Union would be a challenge. There was the danger that Southern state governments might be led by ex-Confederates anxious to undo what the war had accomplished. In 1865, Congress met with the intention of taking charge of the president's Reconstruction program, convinced that he was not getting the job done. However, the South sent some interesting representatives to Congress: the former vice president of the Confederacy, four Confederate generals, five Confederate colonels, six Confederate cabinet officers, and fifty-eight members of the Confederate Congress. They couldn't take the oath of office, but their election showed that the South was standing behind its defeated leaders. There were other decisions to be made, too. Should the welfare of freed African Americans, who were in dire need of help, be attended to before the Southern states were allowed back in the Union? And how could the government manage the general climate of hate?

The Nature of Freedom

The Thirteenth Amendment did not grant freedmen (ex-slaves) citizenship or the right to vote. It's important to remember that abolitionists (people who fought to end slavery) were not automatically in favor of voting rights for black people. Only the "radical" faction of the Republican Party supported the idea of full political equality for blacks, and they felt that way only because black support in elections would make sure that the Republicans had control over the Southern states. Other parts of the country were experiencing a large influx of African Americans for the first time and reacted by voting against black suffrage in Connecticut, Michigan, Wisconsin, Ohio, Kansas, and Minnesota, or ignoring the issue in other states.

After the abolition of slavery, there were suddenly four million blacks in the United States without any experience of public affairs, and millions of immigrants from Europe, most of whom had never participated in government in any way. They didn't speak English and they had no education. Corrupt politicians took advantage of these new arrivals, and also of country people who had been attracted to the affluence of the cities.

African Americans Demand Their Rights

Ex-slaves began to search for their husbands, wives, and children, trying to unite families that had been torn apart by slavery. They did whatever was required to make their marriages legal and their children "legitimate" in the eyes of the law. Blacks were afraid that they might slip into a life not much better than their lives as slaves, particularly after the death of President Lincoln in 1865.

21

The Right to Vote

In that year, blacks held conventions with the idea that they could make plans to improve their lives in America. A convention in Nashville, Tennessee, protested the state's failure to pass fair laws protecting African Americans, and demanded that Congress recognize black citizenship. In Raleigh, North Carolina, a group of 120 African Americans announced that they wanted fair wages, education for their children, and a repeal of discriminatory laws that had been passed by the state legislature. Blacks in Mississippi protested reactionary policies in their state and asked Congress for voting rights. The same demand was made in Charleston, South Carolina, and Mobile, Alabama.

While the South was losing the war, the North had become industrialized. Railroads had spread out, connecting northern states to the West, and steel factories were producing more than had been needed for the war. Wartime profiteers, bankers, and industrialists began to manage political affairs after the war. America was soon a hotbed of corruption and conflict between western farmers and eastern money men.

Aside from ensuring that the Southern states would comply with the changes taking place, the Northern states wanted to punish the South. Members of Congress who wanted to maintain strict control over the South enacted the Wade-Davis Bill. It took away voting rights from all former Confederate soldiers and confiscated certain property in an effort to shift political control of the South away from the big plantation owners and over to the small farmers and craftsmen.

Most Southern states had abolished slavery with the ratification of the Thirteenth Amendment to the Constitution.

After emancipation, many black people had no choice but to work for their former masters, helping to reestablish the South's agrarian economy.

But these states also enacted laws that violated the civil rights of black people, called "Black Codes," which were strikingly similar to the slave codes used to punish slaves and keep them tied to their owners. They also elected to state and federal office many of the ex-Confederates whose voting rights had been taken away.

The Black Codes attacked the freedoms of African Americans in different ways. While in the South the right of blacks to be free to work for money was recognized, their right to refuse work often was not. The Black Codes were designed largely to force ex-slaves to accept low wages in jobs they could not quit. Many blacks, both men and women, found themselves with no choice but to work for their former "masters," helping to reestablish the agrarian (farm-based) economy of the South. Cotton and sugar did well, but free black workers did not. In the sharecropping

23

system that replaced slavery, the costs of farming were so high that by the end of the year, many ex-slaves owed all of what they'd earned to their employers. Landlords provided land, seed, and credit. Farmers, or croppers, would work the land for a share in the profits from the sale of the crop, minus what they owed the landlord. White landlords demanded payment for all sorts of things from their black workers, so that debts exceeded earnings, and those who owed their landlords were tied to working the land just as if they had been slaves.

Some laws tried to limit areas in which blacks could rent or own property. Some codes prohibited black people from just standing around in public. This was designed to force blacks to work. White employers treated their black employees much like slaves, forcing them to sign employment contracts that made it illegal to quit the job. African Americans could not testify in court unless the case involved another black person. They had to pay fines for making "insulting" gestures, for being absent from work, for violating curfew, or for possessing firearms. They did not have the right to vote, nor did it look as if they ever would.

The Southern Homestead Act of 1866 opened public lands in Alabama, Mississippi, Louisiana, Florida, and Arkansas to all settlers, regardless of race. Eighty acres were available to the head of each family. The government did not hand out "forty acres and a mule," as is widely believed, but African Americans were acquiring land wherever they could in an effort to earn economic security.

In business and industry, however, blacks were often used by bosses to undermine white workers' demands for improved working conditions such as an eight-hour workday.

Bosses displaced white workers by hiring cheaper black labor. Black and white workers, therefore, were not going to unite to confront management. Blacks were not particularly welcome in labor organizations or at their meetings.

The Reconstruction Act of 1867

Radical Republicans in Congress, led by Thaddeus Stevens, refused to allow the participation of the ex-Confederate Southern representatives, and they passed Reconstruction acts that would change the way things were done in the South, over the president's veto (rejection). They did this to protect the rights of African Americans and to prevent the Democrats from gaining control of the South. Support for universal suffrage (voting for all men, regardless of race) was thin, and the Republicans lost many seats in Congress in 1867. To maintain some control of the government, they nominated Ulysses S. Grant for president, instead of Chief Justice Salmon Chase, who was a supporter of black suffrage. The Republicans also passed the Reconstruction Act of 1867.

Under the Reconstruction Act, the South (except for Tennessee) was divided into five military districts in which the army governed civil affairs. Each Southern state was required to hold a convention to create a new state constitution. The constitutions were to include universal male suffrage and had to be approved by Congress for the state to be admitted back into the Union. In addition, any state that did not ratify the Fourteenth Amendment would not be

25

allowed into the Union. Former Confederate rebels were disenfranchised. President Andrew Johnson vetoed this bill, but Congress overrode his veto and took further measures to advance their program for Reconstruction.

The Republican Bid for Power

Later in 1867, the Republicans realized that they could probably count on the black vote, so they began to campaign for black support. In 1868, the year in which the Fourteenth Amendment giving civil rights to blacks was passed, the Republicans still made a weak showing at the polls. The *Philadelphia Press* made a public call for a Fifteenth Amendment to give black men the right to vote. Republicans saw black suffrage as the only way for their party to survive. President Johnson opposed these measures. He favored home rule for the states, and didn't believe that the federal government should interfere with the way each state chose to govern its people. Johnson also defied the Tenure of Office Act, an act that required the president to get the approval of the Senate before removing anyone from a federal office who'd been approved by the Senate to begin with. The act was passed to prevent Johnson from ending the military occupation of the Southern states. In 1868 he was impeached (charged with a crime) by Congress, but not removed from office. His violation of the Tenure of Office Act was the main formal charge against him, though Republicans were really upset with his failure to support their Reconstruction policies.

African American Women

Black women also took part in the struggle for civil rights and voting rights, despite the fact that they would not win the right to vote themselves for some time to come. Women founded clubs and organizations that dealt with problems of literacy, health, economics, and politics. They created educational institutions and attacked segregation and discrimination.

Ida B. Wells Barnett was a newspaper reporter, a member of the Afro-American Council, and a founder of the British Anti-Lynching Society, the NAACP, the Negro Fellowship League, and the National Association of Colored Women. Her autobiography is called *Crusade for Justice*.

The changes taking place in the South were difficult for white conservatives to bear. Many white men were losing their voting rights as black men gained theirs. African Americans in the District of Columbia were given the vote. The plan to reconstruct the South through severe treatment was moving forward, and other plans were being hatched to get the president out of office. The abolitionists, politicians, and industrialists had triumphed. They all looked to gain something through Reconstruction.

The Freedmen's Bureau

The Freedmen's Bureau was established in 1865 and had officials in each of the Southern states. Its purpose was to help former slaves by providing them with supplies and

27

medical services, establishing schools, supervising contracts between ex-slaves and their employers, and managing confiscated or abandoned land, leasing and selling some to former slaves. In the North, the Bureau was considered too expensive to support during peacetime. The South objected to it for political reasons. They feared that the bureau's plans to give blacks the vote would lead to a strong Republican hold over the South.

Black Participation in Politics

African Americans were becoming very active politically. The constitutional conventions called for by the 1867 Reconstruction Act all had black participants. In most states (except South Carolina and Louisiana) blacks were, in number, a respectable minority. Some had been slaves, but some had always been free, including some that had come down from the North. They took part in government and argued for universal voting rights. Beverly Nash, a former slave who was elected to the South Carolina Constitutional Convention, said:

> I believe, my friends and fellow-citizens, we are not prepared for this suffrage. But we can learn. Give a man tools and let him commence to use them, and in time he will learn a trade. So it is with voting. We may not understand it at the start, but in time we shall learn to do our duty.

The state constitutions that were written in 1867 and 1868 were very progressive (forward-moving) for the South. Property qualifications for voting and holding office were abolished. Some states got rid of laws that imprisoned people for debt. All states abolished slavery, and some tried to end race distinctions in the possession of property. In every state the ballot was extended to all male residents, except to certain groups of ex-Confederates. Some blacks actually openly opposed the disqualification of Confederates, including P.B.S. Pinchback, the first African American state governor, and Beverly Nash, who went on to say at the convention:

We recognize the Southern white man as the true friend of the black man . . . In these public affairs we must unite with our white fellow-citizens. They tell us that they have been disfranchised, yet we tell the North that we shall never let the halls of Congress be silent until we remove that disability.

The Fourteenth Amendment

Congress, led by radical Republicans, reacted to the Southern states' refusal to extend suffrage to blacks by passing, over President Johnson's veto, the Civil Rights Act of 1866. The act anticipated the Fourteenth Amendment by making United States citizens of all native-born people except untaxed Native American Indians. It guaranteed to African Americans the right to enforce contracts, file lawsuits, testify in court, own property, and enjoy all the benefits of law that whites enjoyed.

Led by the famous black abolitionist Frederick Douglass and George Downey, blacks continued to lobby Congress for voting rights, but the decision on suffrage was left up to the states in Section Two of the Fourteenth Amendment. It was feared that the North would reject black suffrage, and therefore the entire amendment, so the decision went back to the states just to get the amendment through. The South remained under military rule for quite a while because so many states refused to ratify the Fourteenth Amendment.

Many thought that blacks should get the vote eventually. Even Thaddeus Stevens believed this: "I do not therefore want to grant them [blacks] this privilege [the vote] for some years . . . four or five years hence, when the freedmen shall have been made free indeed, when they shall have become intelligent enough." In 1863, Frederick Douglass had this to say to a meeting of the Anti-Slavery Society:

> I understand the antislavery societies of this country to be based on two principles . . . first, the freedom of the blacks of this country; and second, the elevation of them . . . It is said that we are ignorant; I admit it. But if we know enough to be hung, we know enough to vote. If the Negro knows enough to pay taxes to support the Government, he knows enough to vote. If he knows enough to shoulder a musket and fight for the flag, fight for the Government, he knows enough to vote.

Douglass was referring to the 37,000 blacks who had died in the Civil War for the Union. When the war ended he pleaded with the society to continue its work, as he believed its job was not done: "Without [the vote] his liberty is a mockery... for in fact if he is not the slave of an individual master, he is the slave of society." Reconstruction had allowed military authorities to register more than 800,000 blacks to vote, greater than the number of Southern whites registered.

Frederick Douglass

Frederick Douglass was born into slavery in Maryland in 1817. He escaped in 1838. In 1845, he published an autobiography that revealed the name of his master, so he hid in England until his freedom could be bought. In America, he published *The North Star,* an abolitionist journal. Douglass also supported women's rights. During the Civil War, he helped recruit black soldiers for the Union army. After the war, he supported Reconstruction. In his lifetime, he held a number of government jobs, the last as minister to Haiti.

The Black Churches

Black churches, which began to grow and expand rapidly after the Civil War, offered a lot of relief to their communities. The churches became a real force as they gained in membership, influence, and organization. Two examples were the African Methodist Episcopal Church, which grew in membership by 55,000 from 1856 to 1866, and the black Baptist churches, which organized the first state convention of blacks in North Carolina. The churches were the first social institutions in the United States to be controlled by African Americans. They served as community service centers, educational centers, and assembly halls for protest and political meetings. In the South there were more severe restrictions on the activities of black churches, especially in rural areas. The church gave blacks the opportunity to develop a leadership, and some of the names that stand out most from this period of history are those of ministers, like Bishop H.M. Turner, who spoke out for black emigration back to Africa, Reverend R.H. Cain, and Bishop J.W. Hood.

African Americans in Office

During Reconstruction, blacks held public office in Southern states. In South Carolina, African Americans had a lot of influence. In the first legislature, there were eighty-seven blacks and forty whites. Jonathan Jasper Wright was the first African American elected to the Pennsylvania bar in 1866. He went to South Carolina, where he was elected to the state Supreme Court. He served from 1870–1876. Other officeholders included Lieutenant Governors Alonzo J. Ransier and Richard H. Gleaves; Samuel J. Lee and Robert B. Elliott; John Roy Lynch, who was elected to the Mississippi state legislature in 1869 and became speaker in 1872 before serving three terms in the U.S. House of Representatives; and Francis L. Cardozo.

Between 1869 and 1901, two African Americans served in the Senate and twenty served in the House of Representatives. The high point of this representation was in the 43rd and 44th Congresses, when seven black men sat in the House of Representatives. All seven were deeply involved with civil rights and education legislation, but they also fought for local improvements for their districts.

The Fifteenth Amendment

In response to black voting rights gained during Reconstruction, whites resorted to violence and formed societies such as the Ku Klux Klan to keep blacks from voting. Congress responded to the chaos that was taking place in the South with the Fifteenth Amendment, guaranteeing blacks the right to vote. It wasn't easy to pass. Debates raged over who should have control over voting rights, the states or the federal government. To amend the Constitution, a two-thirds majority vote on the amendment is required in both the Senate and the House of Representatives. Then the amendment must be ratified by three-quarters of the states. As a result, the Fifteenth Amendment went through different forms before the House and Senate passed it in 1869. The version that was officially given to the states to ratify stated: "The right of citizens of the United States to vote shall not be denied or abridged by the United States or by any state on account of race, color, or previous condition of servitude. The Congress shall have the power to enforce this article by appropriate legislation." There was no mention of the right to hold office, and it didn't forbid the sorts of things that could and would keep people from the polls, like literacy tests and property requirements.

Now the amendment had to be passed in three-quarters of the existing twenty-six states. Southerners realized that they still had many ways open to them to disqualify blacks from voting, so those states didn't present too much of a problem. In the West, the amendment was unpopular because it would also give the vote to the many Chinese

The Ku Klux Klan, who used brute force to keep blacks from voting, had a membership that included some of the most respectable members of white society, including lawyers, ministers, and doctors.

immigrants who lived there. But by the end of March 1869, three-quarters of the states had voted in favor of the amendment, and it became law. In an address to the nation, President Ulysses S. Grant said:

> A measure which makes at once four millions of people voters, who were heretofore declared by the highest tribunal in the land not citizens of the United States, nor eligible to become so . . . is indeed a measure of grander importance than any other one act of the kind from the foundation of our free government to the present day.

But trouble still lay ahead. In 1870 Congress passed the first Force Act. Elections were to be overseen by federal forces. The law spelled out dozens of types of interference with the civil and political rights of blacks that had been taking place, and which would from then on be considered crimes. Despite the newest amendment, African Americans' voting rights continued to be violated. Interest in black rights began to weaken as the country grew and business and industry changed the face of the nation. Many felt that the passage of the Fifteenth Amendment had given blacks all they needed to fend for themselves. In southern states, laws that were passed to protect blacks were regularly and openly defied. To discourage black voters or make their votes useless, they were required to pay poll taxes, had to meet property qualifications, and were subject to violence, including murder. The number of polling places was reduced in some areas, and Democrats also engaged in gerrymandering, establishing election district borders to benefit their party.

Secret Societies

Southern white leaders relied on the tactics of white supremacist societies to gain control over blacks and take away their power. The most powerful of these secret societies were the Knights of the White Camellia and the Ku Klux Klan. These groups were armed and used any method they liked to deprive blacks of political equality. They committed murder, used force and intimidation, and set fires. Blacks who disobeyed the order not to vote were run out of their communities, whipped, and hanged. Black officials were pushed out of office with terrifying threats. Congress passed laws in 1870 and 1871 to try to suppress these activities, and many people were arrested, but it did not bring an end to the hatred and violence.

The Ku Klux Klan, whose purpose was to drive away or kill leading blacks and any whites who helped them, had a membership that was often made up of the most respectable members of white society: lawyers, ministers, doctors, and others. Blacks who held political office were running a great risk. Charles Caldwell was an African American state senator from Mississippi who was brutally murdered by the Klan. The Klan used brute force to prevent blacks from voting or having any real place in society. They burned schools and tortured and killed teachers. The number of blacks killed by the Klan during Reconstruction alone is estimated at 20,000 to 40,000. The violence convinced Congress to pass Force Acts in 1870, 1871, and 1872. If blacks were to vote, they'd need federal force for protection. By 1872, there was a decrease in Klan violence as a result of these acts.

The Failure of Reconstruction

Southern states refused to uphold the indictments of Klansmen in court. By 1874, the federal government was doing almost nothing to curb the Klan. In 1875, roaming mobs of armed whites killed hundreds of blacks suspected of Republican sympathies. The day before elections, they rode around announcing that they'd kill any blacks who showed up to vote. Not even the Republicans, longtime supporters of black causes, were fighting against the rabid southern Democrats any more. In that same year, Congress passed its last civil rights act for nearly 100 years. It prohibited race discrimination in hotels, railroads, restaurants, and other places of "public accommodation." No effort was made to enforce this act, and it was declared unconstitutional by the Supreme Court in 1883. By 1885 most southern states required separate schools for white and black children, by law. In 1896 the Supreme Court upheld segregation with its "separate but equal" doctrine (*Plessy v. Ferguson*). The twentieth century began in the South with an atmosphere of hate and tension in which all institutions—schools, courts, and the law—favored whites.

Reconstruction had failed to provide economic security for ex-slaves, making it very easy for Southern whites to overthrow Reconstruction and restore their white supremacist system. In their efforts to win political power in the South, the Democrats and Republicans failed to establish peace not just between the North and the South, but also between the races. The people in power had had enough of Reconstruction.

Rutherford B. Hayes, candidate for the presidency, promised he would end the program, and he did. Shortly after he was elected, he pulled the last federal troops out of the South. In 1878, the use of army personnel was forbidden.

Reconstruction came to an end gradually, as many ex-Confederates regained the right to vote and Democrats began to take over the South. It was soon possible for the South to rule itself as it had before the Civil War. The North became less interested in the crusade for black rights, and focused more on the industrial interests of the country as a whole. People more interested in profits slowly replaced radical Republicans.

The Fifteenth Amendment had said that no state could deny a citizen's right to vote, but it did not say anything about what individuals might do. As blacks watched their voting rights slip away, other hard-won rights also seemed to be disappearing, particularly with the introduction of "Jim Crow" laws in the southern states. These laws enforced separation in railroads, streetcars, depots, waiting rooms, theaters, hotels, barbershops, and restaurants. Black facilities were almost always inferior to those provided for whites.

States wrote new constitutions or amended old ones to include property-owning qualifications for voters. Voters had to provide evidence of good character and three to five years of steady employment. Some voters were given literacy tests. The applicant had to interpret or read long passages from the state's constitution to the satisfaction of his examiner. Voter registration and a poll tax were required months ahead of the election. A receipt showing that the tax had been paid had to be presented at the polling place. Grandfather clauses were reintroduced to protect illiterate whites. A grandfather clause meant that a person could cast his vote only if his grandfather had been able to do so in the past. There were also all-white primaries. A primary is an election held by a political party to choose a candidate. Since a primary was not, technically, considered an official state or federal election, it was not covered by the Fifteenth Amendment. In the South, voting in primaries was restricted to whites. Blacks could not nominate or vote for anyone, black or white, sympathetic to their situation.

There were other sneaky ways to keep blacks from voting. Aside from threats of violence, polling places were moved, or the only way to get to them would be mysteriously blocked, with ferries out of order. Often the polling place was just too far away from the black community. When these things didn't work, whites simply barred the entrances, telling black voters to go home. Carl Shurz, a leading abolitionist, said of the South,

Men who are honorable in their dealings with their white neighbors, will cheat a Negro without feeling a single twinge of their honor. To kill a Negro they do not deem murder ... to take away property from a Negro, they do not consider robbery.

At the turn of the century, W.E.B. Du Bois and other northern black professionals began a movement to fight for voting rights. If blacks were to advance in society in any way, they argued, they needed to be able to vote. Not all black leaders agreed. Booker T. Washington did not speak out against the new southern state constitutions. He wanted African Americans to concentrate on education and economic independence and forget about politics. Gradually, northern whites got involved in the voting rights

39

movement. By 1910 the movement became an official organization called the National Association for the Advancement of Colored People (NAACP).

The NAACP began its fight in the courts. In 1915, the Supreme Court ruled that grandfather clauses were unconstitutional. By 1916, the court had also ruled against other regulations designed to keep blacks from voting. By the 1920s the number of blacks voting began to increase. There were more "open elections," or elections outside the white primary system. Black leaders emerged, as well, but from the 1920s to the 1930s the number of blacks voting was still very small. In the 1930s, President Franklin Roosevelt's New Deal included an agricultural program. Black tenant farmers and sharecroppers were given the right to vote on yearly crop issues. For many black farmers, it was their first ballot. In 1944, the Supreme Court brought an end to white primaries. In 1948, black voters played an important role in Harry Truman's victorious run for the presidency. The 1950s saw the end of the poll tax, but still over 75 percent of voting-age blacks were not even registered.

Despite the many battles fought, African Americans would not be able to fully exercise their rights for years to come. Here you've seen how difficult it was to pass laws that protected African Americans. They lived in a society that was convinced of their innate inferiority. It was almost impossible to overcome such a social structure, particularly in the South at this time. Changing a society's notions about a group of people is an uphill battle. It seems that before we can claim our rights, we have to teach others what our rights are. Women faced a similar struggle as their roles in American society changed.

3 Women and the Right to Vote

Today, women wear pants. They expect to work for paychecks made out in their own names and not those of their husbands. They assume that they will automatically be the guardians of their own children. Women serve on juries, get law degrees, and testify in court. They go to college and graduate school. They are the presidents of large companies and they are elected officials. There once were many people who worked very hard to change a world that did not consider women to be intelligent, responsible people who could make good decisions about who should run their country.

Early American Feminists

Many people believe that the fight for women's rights began in the late 1800s and stopped after the 1960s, but in truth women were demanding equality in America as early as the 1600s, and they continue to fight for equal treatment today. The struggle for equal rights for women began long before

41

all the marches, speeches, conventions, and demands for a constitutional amendment. One of the country's first known feminists (a person who believes that women have the same rights that men have) was Anne Hutchinson, who came to the Massachusetts colony from England in 1634. She came looking for religious freedom. During the long trip from England, she gathered around her other women to talk about the sermons that the group's ministers preached. She was allowed to continue this fairly unusual activity as long as she didn't question the men's ideas or their authority. After she arrived in Massachusetts, she held meetings in her home twice a week, eventually developing a following that included men. She was arrested, tried, excommunicated from the Puritan Church, and banished from the Massachusetts colony. She was the first woman in America to raise the issue of women's rights, and had created what was, in a way, the first opposition political party. She, her family, and her followers traveled to Rhode Island, where they founded the city of Portsmouth.

Another early American feminist was Margaret Brent, who came to the Maryland colony from England in 1638 with her sister and brothers. She became a very close friend of Governor Leonard Calvert, the younger brother and representative of Lord Baltimore in England. When Calvert died, it was found that he had named her his only executor (the person in charge of making sure the requests in a person's will are granted). She was in charge of his estate, and took the job seriously. She took over his house and property, as well as his position as Lord Baltimore's agent. That meant that she had a lot of authority in the colony: She controlled the money, collected taxes, and paid the colony's

Suffragists met at the summer headquarters of the Congressional Union for Women's Suffrage in Newport, Rhode Island.

employees. When the House of Burgesses, the first law-making assembly in America, met in 1648, she shocked them by showing up to demand the right to sit with them and vote. She wanted two votes—one as Calvert's executor, and one as Lord Baltimore's representative. She didn't get what she wanted, but she had won the respect of many.

The Antislavery Movement and Women's Rights

In the early nineteenth century, there was a growing dissatisfaction among women about their lives. Lucretia Mott, Elizabeth Cady Stanton, Angelina Grimké, Lucy Stone, and Susan B. Anthony all fought hard for women's rights and women's education. Some women began to speak publicly

43

about moral reform, presenting themselves as guardians of morality. They wanted to govern the behavior of the entire country with a strict interpretation of Christian scriptures. But the Female Reform Society did not evolve into a feminist program. Its emphasis was on purifying American sexual behavior, and its members were not prepared to disregard a woman's role in the home. They criticized men for taking away women's power, but they limited their attack to "male tyranny in the home department." These reformers weren't ready to say that women should have total authority over their own lives.

Those women who joined the American Antislavery Society of William Lloyd Garrison, on the other hand, learned about politics in a way that made them more aggressive. They learned a new way of looking at the world and developed tactics for changing it. The abolitionists taught women what to do with their feelings of oppression. As more women joined the political battle to abolish slavery, they learned how to fight for their own equality. It was considered unwomanly and shameless for a woman to speak in public, yet many women began to do so, to the sound of jeers and shouts.

Women's Right to Fight

It is hard for us today to imagine how difficult it was for women to speak out about what they believed in. But nineteenth century American society was governed by rules derived from a very conservative interpretation of Christian scriptures. Ministers preached that the Bible instructed women to keep silent. As a result, it was not easy for women to participate in antislavery societies and other activities along with men, and so many formed their own organizations. One such woman was Mary S. Parker, who left her home in Boston to run the Women's Anti-slavery Convention in New York in 1837. This meeting attracted 200 delegates from nine states, some of whom were free black women. The next year, the meeting, in Philadelphia this time, was brought to an end by an angry shouting mob. To keep the women as safe as she could, Maria Weston Chapman, that year's leader, led the women out of the hall with a white woman holding the hand of each black woman. After the women got out, the mob set fire to the meeting hall.

It was from antislavery groups such as these that women traveled to the World Anti-Slavery Convention in London, England, in the summer of 1840. They were not welcomed warmly. As the women sat silently, their right to participate was hotly debated by the men, many of whom were clergymen. Some were on the side of the women. A legislator from Massachusetts, George Bradburn, was so frustrated by the end of the day that he said, "Prove to me, gentlemen, that your Bible sanctions the slavery of women—the complete subjugation of one-half the race to the other—and I should feel that the best work I could do for humanity would be to make a grand bonfire of every Bible in the Universe." In the end it was decided that the women could stay, but they could not speak, nor could they sit with the men. They were forced to sit in a gallery behind a curtain. Something very important came out of that seating arrangement, however. The women's section made it possible for Elizabeth Cady Stanton to meet Lucretia Mott. Mott was well known, particularly in women's circles, for her commitment to the cause of abolition. She did not wear any clothes made of cotton and she did not serve coffee, sugar, or rice in her home, because these products depended on the labor of slaves. Stanton, young and newly married, was thrilled to meet her. They became friends, and, no doubt inspired in part by the curtain in front of them, they resolved that they would set up their own convention to fight for the rights of women.

Seneca Falls, 1848

WOMEN'S RIGHTS CONVENTION!

A convention to discuss the social, civil and religious condition and rights of woman, will be held in the Wesleyan Chapel, at Seneca Falls, N.Y., on Wednesday and Thursday, the 19th and 20th of July, current; commencing at 10 o'clock, AM.

During the first day the meeting will be exclusively for women, who are earnestly invited to attend. The public generally are invited to be present on the second day, when Lucretia Mott of Philadelphia, and others, ladies and gentlemen, will address the convention.

This small ad, which appeared in the Seneca County Courier on July 14, 1848, lit a spark that began the movement for the rights of women. The convention was the first time that Elizabeth Cady Stanton spoke publicly. She offered up her "Declaration of Sentiments," modeled after

Lucretia Mott

Born in Massachusetts, Lucretia Mott was raised as a Quaker and developed her public speaking skills by speaking at Quaker meetings. In the 1830s, Mott introduced the idea that slavery was a sin. With Elizabeth Cady Stanton, she planned the first women's rights convention, where she delivered the opening and closing addresses. Lucretia Mott dedicated her life to abolition and women's rights, harboring runaway slaves at her home in Philadelphia and fighting for black suffrage and education after emancipation.

Jefferson's Declaration of Independence. She charged that men had systematically denied women their rights. She addressed the crowd:

> We are assembled to protest against a form of government existing without the consent of the governed—to declare our right to be free as man is free, to be represented in the government which we are taxed to support, to have such disgraceful laws as give man the power to chastise and imprison his wife, to take the wages which she earns, the property which she inherits, and, in case of separation, the children of her love; laws which make her the mere dependent on his bounty. It is to protest against such unjust laws as these that we are assembled today, and to have them, if possible, forever erased from our

statute books, deeming them a shame and a disgrace to a Christian republic in the nineteenth century . . . We now demand our right to vote according to the declaration of the government under which we live . . . The right is ours. The question now is: how shall we get possession of what rightfully belongs to us? . . . The right is ours. Have it, we must. Use it, we will.

Stanton offered eleven resolutions to be ratified by the convention. Ten of them passed immediately; the eleventh, above, was a demand for women's suffrage. This was a very startling demand. Most people had never considered this possibility. Stanton's fellow organizers were worried. This was such an unusual demand that they feared that the entire convention would be ridiculed. Frederick Douglass, the famous African American abolitionist, stood up for Stanton's eleventh resolution. He believed that women had to have the vote if they had any hope of changing the laws that treated them so unfairly:

All that distinguishes man as an intelligent and accountable being is equally true of woman. And if that government only is just which governs by the free consent of the governed, there can be no reason in the world for denying to woman the exercise of the elective franchise.

Douglass' speech helped the resolution on woman suffrage to pass. *The North Star*, Frederick Douglass' Rochester, New York paper, published the first report about the convention at Seneca Falls.

Political Change

The changing social conditions in the America of the early 1800s brought about the conventions, meetings, and protests of women. Women were slowly getting more access to higher education, and more women were becoming politically active over issues such as slavery and temperance (restriction on alcoholic drinks). Eventually, suffrage became the focus of the women's rights movement. The activists knew that once they had the vote, they'd have the power to make other changes and claim more of their rights. These "suffragettes," as they were called, had a lot of opponents. Many men, such as this writer for the *Oneida Whig*, feared that giving women the right to vote would bring an end to family life:

> *This bolt [rebellion] is the most shocking and unnatural incident ever recorded in the history of womanity. If our ladies will insist on voting and legislating, where, gentlemen, will be our dinners and our elbows? Where our domestic firesides and the holes in our stockings?*

Other arguments against women's suffrage included the fear that it would bring socialism to America. Socialism was a bad word in a country full of business owners, who feared radical changes would take place in government because women would make such unpredictable decisions. Another very widespread belief was that the women's movement was a sin against God. Men stood on street corners to shout about it; they handed out pamphlets that warned of "the

49

Dark and Dangerous Side of Woman Suffrage." J.C.
McQuiddy of the *Gospel Advocate* wrote:

> *Everybody knows that men and women are not equal in all
> things. I do not believe that the good women want the bal-
> lot; but even if they did, the question which man must
> determine is not affected by what women want, but by what
> they ought to have . . . If any are disposed to fault with this
> position, they are disposed to complain of the will of God
> Almighty and not the will of man; and that is just what
> Mrs. Catt and the leaders of woman suffrage are doing.*

Elizabeth Cady Stanton and Susan B. Anthony

If Elizabeth Cady Stanton and Susan B. Anthony had not
met, it is hard to say how long women would have waited
for their rights. Never has there been a more powerful pair-
ing of friends, united to fight for one goal. They were two
very different people. Stanton was born into wealth and was
lively, witty, and married. Anthony was a Quaker who had
chosen not to marry. She was more of a strategist and very
plainspoken. They sustained the woman's movement that
changed America forever. Anthony believed that "the true
woman will . . . be her own individual self, stand or fall by
her own individual wisdom and strength. She will proclaim
the glad tidings of good news to all women that woman,
equally with man, was made for her own individual happi-
ness, to develop every talent given to her by God in the
great work of life."

Stanton and Anthony lived in a world where women were barred from the pulpit, the professions, and college. They could not own or inherit property; they were the property of their husbands under the law. Husbands were entitled, by law, to their wife's wages and body. Women could not serve on a jury and were considered incompetent to testify. Stanton hated the way things were. She said, "If God has assigned a sphere to man and one to woman, we claim the right ourselves to judge His design in reference to us. We think that a man has quite enough to do to find out his own individual calling without being taxed to find out also where every woman belongs."

The women and their ideas were ridiculed. Despite the hardships, Stanton, Anthony, and the other activists continued their work. They started working on women's issues such as temperance, divorce reform, coeducation, married women's property rights, dress reform, and equal pay for equal work, but eventually shifted their focus to women's suffrage. They were viciously attacked in the press and condemned as heretics.

Stanton Speechifies

When Stanton and Anthony's equal pay proposal came to a vote at a state teacher's convention in Rochester, New York, it was defeated. Most of the women present had voted against it. The outspoken Stanton declared, "What an infernal set of fools these schoolmarms must be. Well, if in order to please men, they wish to live on air, let them. The sooner the present generation of women die out, the better. We have jackasses enough in the world now without such women propagating more." When they began to concentrate on woman suffrage, Stanton had this to say: "Strange as it may seem to many, we now demand our right to vote according to the Declaration of the government under which we live . . . To have drunkards, idiots, horse-racing rum-selling rowdies, ignorant foreigners and silly boys fully recognized, while we ourselves are thrust out from all the rights that belong to citizens, is too grossly insulting to be longer quietly submitted to."

Women for Women

Anthony and Stanton were joined in their crusade by many women. Among them was Lucy Stone, one of the first women to graduate from college and the organizer of a women's convention in Massachusetts. Also involved was Reverend Antoinette Brown, the first woman ordained as a minister in America and an outspoken soldier in the battle for religious equality. There was Sojourner Truth, the ex-slave-turned-abolitionist; and Frances Harper, a free black teacher and writer who was active in the antislavery movement. Truth became well-known for her skill at winning over a crowd with stirring speeches:

> *We'll have our rights, see if we don't. And you can't stop us from them, see if you can. You may hiss as much as you like. But it's coming. We have all been thrown down so long, that nobody thought we'd ever get up again, but we have been long enough trodden now, we will come up again. And now I'm here.*

In 1854, Susan B. Anthony organized a women's rights convention in Albany, New York, to gain support for changes in state laws that discriminated against women. The convention fought for changes in women's property rights and woman suffrage. Stanton's address to the delegates at the convention was aimed at the men of the state legislature. After the convention, Anthony made sure there was a copy of Stanton's speech on the desk of every state lawmaker. A month later, two laws were amended. A woman's right to keep her own earnings was strengthened, and women now had some measure of control over the custody of their children. It was one of the first battles Stanton and Anthony had won. Anthony organized a National Women's Rights Convention every year up to the Civil War in 1861. After the 1854 convention, Anthony traveled to canvass support for women's property rights. Some people went to Anthony's speeches just for the spectacle of a woman speaking in public. Everywhere she went she was yelled at, insulted, abused, and pelted with rotten food.

In 1860, Stanton addressed the Judiciary Committee of the New York State legislature and demanded that women be treated as citizens, not slaves. This, with all the petitions they'd been gathering for six years, helped pass the Married Woman's Property Act. This act gave a wife the right to own property without interference from her husband. She could keep all her own earnings, sue in a court of law, and share custody of her own children. Women in other states got copies of the new law and started pressuring their own state legislatures to pass the same act.

Women Against Women and the Civil War

At the National Women's Rights Convention in New York City, Elizabeth Cady Stanton suggested something that a lot of people were not ready to hear. She challenged the institution of marriage. She demanded divorce rights, saying that marriage should be a purely legal contract. Either party should be free to end the marriage in the case of drunkenness, desertion, or cruelty. This was a shocking idea. Women could not divorce their husbands, no matter how abusive the relationship might be. If a woman got divorced, she might re-marry, and that would mean a relationship with more than one man. It was unheard of. Lucy Stone and other delegates were horrified by Stanton's idea, and wanted her proposal stricken from the agenda. Anthony defended Stanton's position, but it was never voted on. Reforming the marriage relationship would be a source of conflict within the movement for many years. Some believed that marriage should be a legal contract, but others believed that marriage was an institution created by God.

The year that the Civil War began, Elizabeth Cady Stanton wanted to cancel the women's rights convention. She believed that if the movement's activists put all their effort in supporting the Union cause, the Union would support the movement when the war was over. Suspending the movement compromised the gains they'd made. The New York State legislature began to chip away at the Married Women's Property Act. Anthony hadn't wanted to stop, but she gave in. During the war she worked with Harriet Tubman to help runaway slaves. When President Abraham Lincoln's Emancipation Proclamation only freed slaves living within the Confederacy, Anthony and Stanton began fighting for the freedom of all slaves. They agitated for the Thirteenth Amendment, passed in 1865, which abolished slavery.

Surely now, the women thought, the men who fought a war for the freedom and natural rights of human beings would grant women the right to vote. They were wrong. Stanton and Anthony helped their progressive allies to form the American Equal Rights Association, dedicated to voting rights for men and women, black and white. Now they wanted universal suffrage. It became clear, though, that African American men were going to get the vote first. The proposed Fourteenth Amendment contained the word "male" in its declaration of who was a citizen and what citizens' rights were. Stanton and Anthony fought hard to get the language of the Fourteenth Amendment changed, but even their friends told them to wait their turn, that this was "the time of the Negro." For two women who had fought thirty years to win freedom for the slaves, this was too insulting. The Fourteenth Amendment was ratified without change. In Section 2 of the amendment, it is specifically noted that the protection of the law refers only to "any of the male inhabitants" of a state. Women were also split over the question of whether to support the Fifteenth Amendment, which gave blacks the right to vote, but made no mention of sex.

Prejudice was rampant within the women's rights movement, and even those who fought for equality for everyone, and for universal suffrage, showed that they lived in a world divided along lines of race and class. Stanton's frustration over the Fifteenth Amendment erupted in a terrible speech she uttered at the annual convention of the American Equal Rights Association. She insulted the former slaves whose freedoms she had championed, and she suggested that empowering people characterized by ignorance and degradation would create fearful outrages against womanhood. "Sambo," she said, "like the ignorant newcomer, wasn't ready for the vote." Frederick Douglass immediately asked to be heard:

> When there were few houses in which the black man could have put his head, this wooly head of mine found refuge in the house of Mrs. Elizabeth Cady Stanton. There is no name greater than hers in the matter of women's rights and equal rights. But the employment of certain names, such as "Sambo," that I cannot coincide with.

Douglass called for the delegates to rally behind the proposed Fifteenth Amendment, without change. He was asking Stanton and Anthony to defer their dreams—again:

> I do not see how anyone can pretend that there is the same urgency in giving the ballot to woman as to the Negro. When women, because they are women, are hunted down through the cities of New York and New Orleans, when they are the object of insult and outrage at every turn, when their children are not allowed to enter schools, then, they will have an urgency to obtain the ballot equal to our own.

Anthony asked, "Is that not all true about black women?"

"Yes that's all true of black women," Douglass replied, "but not because she is a woman, but because she is black."

Anthony retorted, "When Mr. Douglass tells us that the cause of the black man is so perilous, I tell him, that wronged and outraged as they are by this hateful and mean prejudice against color, he would not today, exchange his sex and color, wronged as he is, with Elizabeth Cady Stanton."

The convention was in turmoil. Lucy Stone was appalled by what Stanton and Anthony had said. Black women delegates were understandably divided. Sojourner Truth, for one, supported Anthony, and Frances Harper sided with Douglass. Eventually the association founded to support universal suffrage voted to support the Fifteenth Amendment, unchanged. The debate over this amendment split the movement, which was terribly damaging. For the movement to succeed, it needed to be radical and unified. Stanton and Anthony realized that they could rely only on themselves. So they formed a radical new organization called the National Woman Suffrage Association (NWSA). Men were not permitted to serve as officers. Within a few months, Lucy Stone, joined by a much larger group of women and men, formed a more conservative association, the American Women's Suffrage Association (AWSA). Anthony and Stanton wanted to fight against the customs and laws of the "Cult of True Womanhood," which confined women to their homes and denied them their rights. They were at war with other women, more conservative than they were over the issues of political strategy, the role of religion, and the unresolved question of race. Old friends were now enemies, and the struggle was divided.

African American Women and Suffrage

In 1895, at the annual Women's Rights Convention in Atlanta, Anthony had gone along with her southern hosts, who wanted to bar black women from the proceedings. Later, she said nothing when the NWSA officially declared that it had no objection to any state preventing black women from joining its local chapters. No one in the center of the movement, therefore, was committed to getting black women the vote. Anthony knew the exclusion was wrong, but she was afraid to risk losing the support of southern white women. She could not afford to alienate a Congress now dominated by white southern men.

Anthony was not alone in this. Other leaders of the women's suffrage movement working with white southerners tried to promote women's suffrage by saying that voting for women, with educational requirements, would limit the vote to white women and therefore help to restore white supremacy in the South. In the South, conservative Democrats, who had defeated African American efforts to vote, were afraid that giving women the vote would reopen the issue of black suffrage. They didn't want to have to go through another period of Reconstruction. Later, in an effort to combat this fear, white suffragists insisted that women's suffrage and black suffrage were unrelated causes.

Black women suffragists in the late nineteenth century wanted to play an active role in the fight for enfranchisement, and had to create their own institutions. White suffragists often used racist tactics, and some excluded black women from membership in their organizations. Just after the Civil War, supporters of the rights of blacks and women worked together for universal suffrage in the American Equal Rights Association. They were divided, though, in 1869, over the exclusion of women from the protections of the Fourteenth and Fifteenth Amendments.

African American women faced a variety of oppressive circumstances. First slavery, then poverty, limited their opportunity to participate in organized women's groups. Southern black women seeking work, running from physical harm, and finding ways to help their families survive couldn't really make the woman suffrage movement a priority. So most black women suffragists seem to have come from a small but growing black middle class. But the changing status of African American women, from slave to free, from rural to urban, from illiterate to literate, encouraged black strategies to achieve women's enfranchisement.

Like white suffragists, African Americans believed that women were treated by society and by the law as second-class citizens, and that they had to win the vote to improve their position in society. By the end of the nineteenth century and the beginning of the twentieth, however, black women began to see suffrage as a way to uplift their race and get their rights. There were a large number of black women suffragists, but most of their words have not been recorded. One who is well known was Sojourner Truth.

Women Warriors

The words of Harriet Forten Purvis and her sister Margaretta Forten were not recorded. They were founding members of the Philadelphia Female Anti-Slavery Society. Abolitionist lecturer Sarah Remond spoke at the National Women's Rights Convention in 1858, but her words were not recorded either. After the Civil War, Hattie Purvis and Frances Ellen Watkins Harper participated in the American Equal Rights Association (AERA). The list of women whose powerful speeches were not written down is long.

The split in the suffrage movement also divided African American women. Some felt that a just amendment was one that granted universal suffrage, while others felt that universal suffrage would have to take place in stages. It would be politically advantageous, they thought, to enfranchise the black man first. Susan B. Anthony and Elizabeth Cady Stanton removed themselves from the "Negro suffrage" issue, believing it would only hurt women's chances. Lucy Stone and Henry Ward Beecher led their followers into AWSA, supporting the Fifteenth Amendment, and allowing men to hold office in the association. Frances Harper thought it was smart to give black men the vote despite the setback to the women's movement. Hattie Purvis attended NWSA meetings, Harper affiliated with AWSA, and Truth attended the meetings of both groups.

Josephine St. Pierre Ruffin was a member of the Massachusetts Woman Suffrage Association. She became a part of that group largely because of the welcome she received from Lucy Stone and other leaders. This may give us an idea why more black women seem to have joined with AWSA rather than NWSA. There were many black women activists. It wasn't until the 1870s that their words, other than those of Sojourner Truth, were written down. Lottie Rollin, the first South Carolina delegate to a

Sojourner Truth

Sojourner Truth was born a slave named Isabella in Ulster County, New York. After slavery was abolished in that state, she did missionary work among New York City's poor. In 1843, she set out on her own as a traveling preacher named Sojourner Truth. Her religious devotion led her to groups of social reformers of the day. She was a wonderful public speaker and lent her talents to both the abolition and women's rights movements. After the Civil War she counseled newly freed slaves in Washington, DC. She also petitioned for public lands to be set aside in the West for a "Negro State." She spent her life speaking out for the rights of the disadvantaged.

women's suffrage convention, addressed the chairman of the South Carolina convention in 1870: "We ask suffrage not as a favor, not as a privilege, but as a right based on the ground that we are human beings, and as such entitled to all human rights."

Black women identified women's suffrage as a potential source of strength to black women during Reconstruction. Frances Harper went to the 1873 AWSA convention in New York, where she told the members that "as much as white women need the ballot, colored women need it more."

Journalist Mary Ann Cary supported the idea that black women's need for the ballot was urgent. In 1880, she organized the Colored Women's Progressive Franchise Association in Washington, DC. Gertrude Bustill Mossell, who was, like Cary, from a prominent family of reformers, started a women's column in T. Thomas Fortune's first newspaper, *The New York Freeman*. In 1896 the National Federation of Afro-American Women merged with the National League of Colored Women to form the National Association of Colored Women (NACW).

All of these women fought for women's rights and the rights of African Americans. At every turn they were met with racism and sexism. Rather than receiving support from white suffragists, they were often excluded from organizations and meetings. They had to fight for their right to vote, even more than white women did. They were able to participate to some degree in national organizations, but by and large they had to create their own organizations and fight their own battles to win their rights. Their battle was doubly difficult, as Frederick Douglass said, because they were black, not because they were women. It wasn't until 1965 that black women were fully franchised, though they were given the right to vote at the same time as white women.

Divided We Stand: The New Women's Movement

Stanton and Anthony's organization, the National Woman Suffrage Association, began to put out a newspaper in 1868 called *The Revolution*. It was staffed completely by women, right down to the typesetters. It had a national distribution, European correspondents, and some of the foremost women writers of the day wrote articles for it. It contained nothing but news about women and the women's rights movement. If a town had its first "postmistress," that made the news. *The Revolution* brought new members to the association, but it failed after only about three years, in part because of *The Woman's Journal*, a paper produced by Lucy Stone and the American Woman Suffrage Association. AWSA was committed to fighting for women's voting rights on a state-by-state basis, while NWSA members fought for the right nationally. They wanted the issue addressed on the federal level.

Taking It to the Courts

Stanton and Anthony pressed on, changing their strategy. If the Fourteenth Amendment was read in a certain way, it could be argued that it gave women their rights. It said, "All persons born or naturalized in the United States and subject to the jurisdiction thereof, are citizens of the United States and of the State wherein they reside. No State shall make or enforce any law which shall abridge the privileges or immunities of citizens of the United States; nor shall any State deprive any person of life, liberty, or property, without due process of law; nor deny to any person within its jurisdiction the equal protection of the laws." This amendment seemed to give women equal rights! Stanton and Anthony decided they would fight their battles in the courts.

With that in mind, on November 1, 1872, Susan B. Anthony and her sisters tried to register to vote in Rochester, New York. Their plan assumed that they would not be allowed to register. Then they would sue the registrars for breaking the law as stated in the Fourteenth Amendment, taking the case all the way to the Supreme Court if need be. But to their surprise, the registrar gave in, so Anthony cast her vote. A few days later, a U.S. marshall came to Anthony's home with a warrant for her arrest. The charge was "knowingly, unlawfully, and wrongfully voting for a representative to the Congress of the United States." Anthony would have to stand trial, and she used this turn of events to get publicity for her cause. They had to move the trial because she'd done so much public speaking about it. The authorities couldn't find a jury that did not already have an opinion about the case.

Because the laws said women were too incompetent to do so, Anthony could not testify on her own behalf. The judge directed the jury to find her guilty. Before he closed the case, he asked Anthony if she had anything to say. That was his mistake. She replied:

I have many things to say. For in your ordered verdict of guilty you have trampled underfoot every vital principle of our government. My natural rights, my civil rights, my political rights are all alike ignored. Robbed of the fundamental privilege of citizenship, I am degraded from the status of a citizen to that of a subject—and not only myself individually, but all of my sex are by your honor's verdict doomed to political subjection under this so-called Republican government.

She refused to be silenced. The judge told her that she'd been tried according to the "established forms of law," but she said:

Yes, your honor. But by forms of law all made by men, administered by men, in favor of men, and against women. And hence your honor's ordered verdict of guilty against a United States citizen for the exercise of that citizen's right to vote simply because that citizen was a woman and not a man.

Anthony was fined $100 plus the costs of prosecution. She said she'd never pay it, and she never did.

A New Battlefield

Anthony's trial reenergized the women's suffrage movement. Stanton and Anthony gave up on the courts and decided that it was time to persuade Congress and the American people. They needed an amendment to the United States Constitution. Then in 1878, Republican Senator Aaron A. Sargent of California proposed a new amendment that would give women the right to vote. It had taken close to three years to find a senator willing to take this step. The day after Sargent made his proposal, Stanton spoke before a Senate committee in support of the proposed amendment. It was a call for federal protection of all citizens, and an indictment of the abuses of civil rights and civil liberties that had come in the wake of *Minor v. Happerset.* She was greeted with derision and disrespect. At least one committee member sat reading his newspaper while she spoke. The amendment never made it out of committee. It would have to be introduced at every session of Congress for the next forty-five years.

Susan B. Anthony stayed on the road, organizing, lecturing, lobbying, and gathering signatures. She had been all over the country and had forged many alliances with a wide variety of groups. This proliferation of women's organizations was one of the most important developments of the late nineteenth century. It brought women into the public eye and developed their leadership.

Anthony continued to narrow her focus to the fight for suffrage. Any issue that divided women needed to be abandoned, she thought, until they'd won the vote. She befriended anyone, even groups that were the enemies of freedom in every other way, who were willing to work for the vote. One example was Frances Willard, president of the Woman's Christian Temperance Union, 200,000 members strong. Willard wanted to extend Christian morality into every aspect of civil life. Small wonder that the owners of liquor businesses did not want to give women the vote; they were sure they'd be put out of business.

In 1888, to honor the fortieth anniversary of the Seneca Falls convention, Anthony organized the International Council of Women in Washington, DC. The council was a success; the women began to work out a merger between the two rival suffrage organizations. Anthony believed that a united movement was the only means to win voting rights. Almost two years later, the two groups united under the National American Women's Suffrage Association (NAWSA). Elizabeth Cady Stanton was elected its first president.

Life for American women had changed dramatically since they'd taken up the fight. Women could attend and graduate from eight out of ten colleges, universities, and professional schools. There were a handful of woman doctors and clergy. Women could own property and keep their earnings, testify in court, and in a few states serve as jurors and practice law. And women had been given the

In honor of the fortieth anniversary of the Seneca Falls convention, Susan B. Anthony organized the International Council of Women in Washington, DC.

right to vote in four western states and territories: Wyoming, Utah, Colorado, and Idaho. It is interesting to note that Utah, which had given women the ballot in the mid-1800s, had to take that right away to be successful in its bid for statehood.

Changes in the Leadership

In 1892, NAWSA held its annual convention in Washington, DC. Now seventy-two years old, Elizabeth Cady Stanton resigned from the presidency. Her farewell speech was called "The Solitude of Self."

> *No matter how much women prefer to lean, be protected and supported, nor how much men prefer to have them do*

so, they must make the voyage of life alone. And for safety in an emergency, they must know something of the laws of navigation. The talk of sheltering women from the fierce storms of life is sheerest mockery, for they beat on her from every point of the compass, just as they do on man, with more fatal results, for he has been trained to protect himself, to resist, to conquer. Whatever the theories may be on woman's dependence on man, in the supreme moments in her life, he cannot bear her burdens. In the tragedies and triumphs of human experience, each mortal stands alone.

Stanton had come to understand that each person, woman or man, is responsible for her or his own life, her or his own actions. The fight for voting rights and other rights for women meant that women might get the opportunity to learn to protect and be responsible for themselves, since in the end, each person "stands alone."

There were new young women to take up the cause who had learned about politics and strategy from Stanton and Anthony. Carrie Chapman Catt, who became president of NAWSA, was one of the women who worked to get voting rights for women through a constitutional amendment. Using many of the methods they'd learned, including marches, petitions, meetings, and much more radical methods, these younger suffragists were not even born when the fight began. Alice Paul, founder of the Women's Party, used hunger strikes and massive marches to make her point.

Into the new century, women battled prejudice from the highest sources. In 1905, President Grover Cleveland took

Carrie Chapman Catt

Carrie Chapman Catt put herself through Iowa State College, and was a principal and school superintendent before she became an activist. She first started lecturing on women's suffrage in Iowa after the death of her first husband, eventually lecturing across the country. When she became head of the National American Women's Suffrage Association in 1915, she put into action a secret and very successful "winning plan": pushing for the Nineteenth Amendment to the constitution while campaigning at the state level. Catt also worked internationally for women's suffrage, traveling to Europe and organizing suffrage groups.

a stand against women's suffrage in the *Ladies Home Journal*. He wrote, "sensible and responsible women do not want to vote. The relative positions to be assumed by man and woman in the working out of our civilization were assigned long ago by a higher intelligence than ours."

Victory

Finally, in 1919, the House of Representatives and the Senate passed the Nineteenth Amendment. The wording matched that of the proposed amendment Stanton and Anthony had submitted forty-five years earlier. Now Catt had to convince thirty-six of the forty-eight states to ratify the amendment. The vote came down to one man, a young representative from Tennessee named Harry Burn. Burn was leaning toward voting it down, but as the story goes, his mother had asked him to be a good boy and pass the amendment. He was, and he did. On November 1, 1920, American women in the millions cast their vote for the first time. They had expanded the franchise and paved the way for the civil rights movement. Sadly, Elizabeth Cady Stanton, Susan B. Anthony, Lucretia Mott, and other women who had devoted their lives to winning these rights did not live to see their dream realized. As Anthony had said, "This is winter wheat we're planting, that others will harvest."

The Struggle Continues

During the nineteenth century, as you've read, the franchise was being expanded. More men were able to cast their votes in an election, and more men were declared citizens of the United States, with the rights of a citizen to be free, to own property, to work for and keep wages, to serve on a jury, and to testify in court. Many women wanted these rights, too. But women were thought of as property, like slaves, but also as incompetent, silly, unintelligent, and needing the sort of care that babies and small children need. They began to fight for suffrage and the other rights of U.S. citizens. The first country to give women the right to vote was New Zealand, in 1893. Women were not given the vote in Switzerland until 1971, and in the tiny country of Liechtenstein, women waited until 1984.

The League of Women Voters was founded in Chicago, Illinois, in 1920. It is dedicated to furthering the development of political awareness through political participation. It is an offshoot of NAWSA, and was formed in the year that women would vote nationally for the first time, in order to educate them in their use of their vote. Today, the league's membership is about 100,000. Men were allowed to join beginning in 1974, and the league's activities focus on any important national political or social concern. It prepares information on candidates and issues, runs voter registration drives, takes stands on pending legislation, and sponsors presidential debates.

In the struggle for suffrage, difficult choices had to be made about whose rights should come first, and what political strategy would have the desired outcome. African American women, for instance, had their hearts in two camps. Nonetheless, as Frederick Douglass pointed out, they were black before they were women in the eyes of racist and sexist lawmakers. African Americans struggled to exercise their right to vote well after the passage of both the Fifteenth and the Nineteenth Amendments. It should be noted, however, that with years of uphill political battles, public humiliation, and abuse behind them, only 49 percent of eligible American women voted in the 1996 presidential election. (Forty-eight percent of men voted in that election.)

4 Young People and the Right to Vote

There have been many restrictions on voting rights in the history of the United States. During the colonial period, a person had to be twenty-one years old to vote, a rule that had been adopted from England. There were colonies whose election laws did not specify a legal voting age, but there were other restrictions that could and did keep people under the age of twenty-one from casting votes.

America at War

One thing becomes very clear when examining the history of voting-age requirements: The argument for the right to vote has been tied to military service since the American Revolution—an idea often called "ballots-for-bullets." The idea is that any person who is willing to defend the government of the United States ought to be given a say about who runs that government and how.

At the time of the Revolutionary War, Thomas Jefferson supported the idea that there were many men wrongly denied the right to vote. He said that the first thing wrong with the constitution of the state of Virginia was that "the majority of men in the state who pay taxes and fight for its support are unrepresented in the legislature, the roll of freeholders [list of landowners] entitled to vote not including generally the half of those on the roll of the militia or of the tax gatherers."

John Adams disagreed. He thought that the vote should go only to those with power and privilege. Changing the rules of voter qualifications, he feared, meant "women will demand a vote [and] lads from twelve to twenty-one will think their rights not enough attended to." Different states had different rules. In some states, a voter was a taxpayer, in others, a landowner, and in others, the age of twenty-one was the only requirement. There were those who argued that all militiamen should have the right to vote, saying that if they were old enough to fight, they were old enough to vote. This debate stood the test of time. It was argued in government offices for nearly two hundred years. The Constitution left the issue of suffrage up to each state.

One of the "problems" with giving the ballot to anyone who had served in the military was that blacks and Native Americans had fought for the country too, and there were even some women who had made great wartime efforts. America was not yet ready to grant blacks, Native Americans, and women the same rights as white men.

The War of 1812

At the time of the War of 1812, America was full of anti-British feelings for many reasons, including the English confiscation of American ships and the impressment (forced enlistment) of American sailors to serve on British ships. The war actually broke out over American expansion into the West, where the British and their Indian allies had claimed the land. And once again, there was a call to give soldiers the right to vote. In 1812, Thomas Jefferson pointed out to the Virginia legislature that in one county there were 1,200 men in the militia, only 200 of whom owned enough property to vote.

The first serious debate about lowering the voting age seems to have taken place in 1820 at the Missouri Convention. Some of the delegates said that socially and economically, every male of eighteen years was doing "a man's work." The proposal to lower the voting age was eventually defeated. In New York in 1821, the idea that a man who was old enough to fight was old enough to vote got a lot of attention. The delegates tried to differentiate between those who'd seen actual combat and those who'd simply worn a uniform. The final vote on the issue was close, but the age was not lowered to eighteen. New York also debated at this time the issue of black suffrage, because even though New York did not allow blacks to join the militia, they had served well in the Revolution and the War of 1812. In 1834, delegates at the Tennessee Convention debated black male suffrage. Blacks not only paid taxes, but had also served in the military. When it seemed as if black men in Tennessee might actually get the vote, a resolution was offered to take the right to vote away from free "colored people" and exempt them from military service.

After the Mexican war of the late 1840s, the unfairness in the treatment of soldiers was becoming a pressing issue. By 1860, there were twenty states that would not extend the ballot to military personnel. The reason for this, argued some state lawmakers, was that soldiers, sailors, and marines often outnumbered the voting population of the town where they were stationed. In seven states, students were not allowed to vote, but in all thirty-four states, three things were true. Native Americans could not vote, women could not vote, and those under twenty-one could not vote.

The Civil War

The "war amendments"—the Thirteenth, Fourteenth, and Fifteenth Amendments—recognized African Americans' contributions to the Civil War. Almost 200,000 blacks had served in the Union army and navy. The Fourteenth Amendment, which gave national citizenship to all people born or naturalized in the United States, recognized another citizenship—that of the state in which a person lives. In addition, Section 2 of the amendment mentions a voter's age for the first time. A state's representation in Congress would be decreased if the vote was "denied to any of the male inhabitants of such State, being twenty-one years of age."

World War I

When the United States declared war on Germany in 1917, it enacted the Selective Service Act, which made all male citizens between the ages of twenty-one and thirty eligible for military service. By 1918, men age eighteen and up had to register for the draft. Registering for the draft did not necessarily mean active military service, but boys as young as fifteen often used their older brothers' names to join the ranks. Many of the servicemen who fought for the United States were Native Americans. In 1919, Congress extended full citizenship to all honorably discharged Indian soldiers and sailors of the war. In 1920, women won their heroic battle for the vote, and in 1924 all Indians, Eskimo peoples, and Aleuts born within the United States were declared citizens.

The Nineteenth Amendment, passed in 1920, said that laws that set down qualifications for voters could not discriminate against women. More people began to argue in favor of extending the vote to the young men who had fought "The Great War." But it was still argued that young minds were immature, not sufficiently experienced in the ways of the world to avoid falling prey to some slick character who might convince them to support evil causes. Like women before them, young people were thought of as unfit, incapable, and incompetent to exercise the right to vote.

World War II

The movement to enfranchise eighteen-to-twenty-year-olds began in earnest at the time of World War II, in 1941. The Selective Training and Service Act of 1940 imposed military service on men between the ages of twenty-one and thirty-six. Eighteen- and nineteen-year-olds were encouraged to volunteer for service. In 1940, President Franklin D.

By 1918, American men ages eighteen and up had to register for the military draft and serve in the armed forces, but they still couldn't vote until they turned twenty-one.

Roosevelt approved a Congressional resolution to set aside the third Sunday in May as a day for public recognition of all who had attained citizenship status. It seemed that the president had indirectly and subtly shown his support for the enfranchisement of eighteen-year-olds.

The Young Voter's League took up the cause for a lower voting age in 1941. In 1942, Congress changed the Selective Service and Training Act, lowering the draft age to eighteen. At this time, one of youth's biggest supporters, Senator Arthur Vandenberg, addressed the Senate. "Mr. President, if young men are to be drafted at eighteen years of age to fight for their Government, they ought to be entitled to vote at eighteen years of age for the kind of government for which they are best satisfied to fight." Then he proposed a constitutional amendment that would change the voting age nationally. He brought the issue up again and again. Representative Jennings Randolph introduced a similar proposal in the House of Representatives. No action was taken before Congress adjourned. So when Congress reconvened in 1943, Senator Vandenberg and Representative Randolph reintroduced their resolutions to Congress. Despite Randolph's enthusiasm and the good arguments he made in favor of lowering the voting age, the resolution did not pass. Randolph would prove to be unwavering in his devotion to this issue. It's also interesting to note a proposal made by Representative Victor Wickersham in 1942. He suggested that the voting age be lowered only for federal elections, creating a system called dual-age voting. What this meant was that young people could vote only in federal elections, for the president for example, but state and local elections would require a minimum voting age of twenty-one.

Another proponent of lowering the voting age at this time was Senator Harley M. Kilgore. In an article in *The American Observer* in 1943, the Senator wrote that if "he's old enough to fight, he's old enough to vote." He could not understand how we could deny a basic right of citizenship to the same people we entrusted with the burdens of warfare, including the risk of death. Still, all efforts to change the voting age on a federal level met defeat. It would, for now, be up to each state to make its own policy.

Georgia, a state that was so strongly against the Nineteenth Amendment that it never ratified it, was the first state to make the change. In 1943, it amended its 1877 constitution to extend to citizens of the United States eighteen years old or more the right to register and vote at any election. The state of Georgia was attacked in the press for its ratification of the amendment. In a statement to *Time* magazine, Governor Herman Talmadge of Georgia responded, "The minimum age to exercise the right of franchise in Georgia was lowered from twenty-one to eighteen during World War II. Those in the General Assembly proposing the move took the position that if a young man was old enough to be drafted to fight for his country then he was certainly old enough to vote. This is an argument which I believe cannot be very successfully refuted."

There were plenty of arguments against connecting the right to vote with military service. An editorial in the *Washington Times-Herald* said that allowing people under twenty-one to vote would clog up the political system with less-experienced, less-wise voters. The editorial argued that there was no rule about being too old to vote even though you can be too old to fight. Nor are women stopped from voting, despite their small number on the battlefield. Georgia did not back down.

W. R. McCarthy was the national secretary-treasurer of American Youth for Democracy in 1944. He sent a powerful letter to the Resolutions and Platform Committee of the Democratic National Convention calling for the inclusion of a lower voting age plank in the party platform. He wanted the issue of voting age to be a deciding factor in the upcoming elections, debated during the campaign. He wrote:

It has been said that those who are old enough to fight are old enough to vote. This has been the soundest argument for wartime action on this proposal. But what of postwar America? It is equally true that after this war is fought and won we want to be able in clear conscience to tell the millions of young men and women now fighting for democracy that the nation they return to extends them a fuller measure of that democracy . . . Immediate action to assure the right to vote to millions of soldiers, sailors, and marines, now eighteen, nineteen, and twenty years of age would, in some measure, eliminate from the record the shameful actions that this year deny the right to vote to untold numbers of qualified voters in the armed forces . . . Young people of voting age and less have an unprecedented interest in all public affairs. This interest grows from knowledge of the fact that youth's own future is being shaped by this war and by our ability to establish a secure postwar world. Youth wants a fair share in shaping that future—not only on the field of battle, but also through our American democratic process. Give youth a chance and it will prove that it fights democracy's battles as well with ballots as it does today with bullets.

There were plenty of people against the proposal. Dr. Kenneth Colsgrove, a professor of political science at Northwestern University, had this to say in a 1943 broadcast debate: "Although eighteen-year-olds know more about the world and its problems than did the twenty-one-year-olds a generation ago, as freshmen and sophomores they are still Republicans or Democrats just because their fathers and mothers were Republicans or Democrats. It is only when young people become seniors or graduate students that they begin to think for themselves and determine their own decisions with reference to political questions."

Post–World War II America

For years to come, proposals for amendments would be brought to Congress, only to be defeated. From 1945 to

President Dwight D. Eisenhower said, "I believe if a man is old enough to fight he is old enough to vote."

1952, nearly one hundred bills proposing a lower voting age were introduced in the legislatures of more than forty states.

In 1951, Representative Edwin Hall introduced a measure that would have given voting rights to all members of the armed forces, regardless of age. Another proposal in 1951 was made by Representative Arthur Klein, which would have lowered the voting age to eighteen throughout the country. These bills were never passed. In 1952, Senator Harley Kilgore introduced a constitutional amendment that would have given voting privileges to all citizens eighteen years of age or over. From 1941 to 1952, there was no positive action on any of the federal proposals that were introduced to lower the voting age.

There was support for the cause, though. The junior equivalents of the American Legion and American Veterans of World War II (AMVETS), and the Veterans of Foreign

The Right to Vote

Wars (VFW) all supported a change in the voting age. The Republican nominee for president, Dwight D. Eisenhower, made his position clear at a press conference in 1952, when he said, "I believe if a man is old enough to fight he is old enough to vote." In the same year, a public opinion poll found that 61 percent of the American people were in favor of a lower minimum voting age, and a *New York Times* poll showed that twenty-nine governors were in favor of such a change.

Support for this cause had increased during the Korean War, and by the end of the war in 1953, letters, petitions, and telegrams were making their way to the offices of Congressmen. During Senate debate in 1953, Senator Hubert Humphrey discussed the qualifications of young people that ought to give them the right to vote. He thought that young people were better educated about the events of the day than they had been in past generations, and that they were likely to be better informed about the issues. He believed that there could be no better civic training than voting itself. It was essential, he said, that young people of the United States take on political responsibility as soon as they were ready, because the "real value of education comes from its association with responsibility." Humphrey concluded, "Youth ought to have a voice in determining its own future. What is more, youth has a definite contribution to make to the future of our whole country. I hope that the Congress will now act to grant suffrage—the most essential right of citizenship—to the youth of America."

In 1953, Republican President Dwight David Eisenhower gave a State of the Union address to Congress in which he endorsed the enfranchisement of

82

eighteen-year-olds. The Republicans were, as a result, look-ing forward to first-time voters being lifetime Republicans. The Republicans were chastised by Congressman Clyde Doyle in his speech to the House of Representatives. He said, "While we can all appreciate the anxiety of the vice president and of the chairman of the Republican National Committee to hope that a great majority of the eighteen-year-olds of America would register with that particular political party, I submit that no such premise should become the basis upon which the American people are asked to amend the Constitution of the United States." In other words, if the only reason that someone votes yes for youth enfranchisement is to get young voters' allegiance to a particular political party, that is not a good reason to make a change to the Constitution.

A 1954 editorial in the *Washington Star* expressed the opinion that the voting age was still a matter of states' rights. Why, the editor wanted to know, would the president, who stood up for state's rights on other issues, want to push it aside for just this one cause? The matter is not urgent, the editorial went on to say. The country will survive if young people have to wait a bit longer. In addition, service to the country in a military capacity, it said, did not in any way qualify a person to vote.

Despite opposition, President Eisenhower was still on the side of youth. In 1954, he spoke to Congress in his State of the Union address: "For years our citizens between the age of eighteen and twenty-one have, in time of peril, been summoned to fight for America. They should participate in the political process that produces this fateful summons. I urge Congress to propose to the

States a constitutional amendment permitting citizens to vote when they reach the age of eighteen." Former first lady Eleanor Roosevelt wrote, "eighteen seems to me a proper voting age. If young people can be drafted at that age, they should also have the right to vote." The Senate failed to pass a resolution for the amendment. Most of the opposition came from southern Democrats, who supported lowering the voting age but wanted it left up to the individual states to decide.

A New Way to Make a Point

Around this time, the American Institute of Public Opinion conducted a nationwide political "quiz" in an effort to determine who was the most politically informed, adults or youths. The quiz was made up of seven questions. Adult voters and young people between the ages of eighteen and twenty, all across the country, tried to answer the questions.

1. How many states will elect members of the United States House of Representatives this fall?
2. How many United States senators are from your state?
3. Can you recall the names of your senators?
4. What is meant by the electoral college?
5. What are the first ten amendments to the Constitution called?
6. What are the three branches of the federal government called?
7. What is the purpose of the Bricker Amendment?

The results were interesting. People in the eighteen-to-twenty group scored an average of 41 percent correct answers. The average of correct answers among people twenty-one or older was 28 percent. It seems there was something to the idea that young people were the better informed group.

Changes on the Horizon

Kentucky, a state that had rejected the Thirteenth, Fourteenth, and Fifteenth Amendments, extended the vote to eighteen-to-twenty-year-olds in 1954. There was very little opposition. An editorial in the *Louisville Courier-Journal* pointed out, though, that "giving the vote to eighteen-year-olds . . . raises a host of legal questions. Twenty-one is not only the legal age for voting, but for negotiating contracts, owning property, marrying without parental consent, and managing personal affairs. Giving eighteen-year-olds one of these rights of majority without conferring on them the other rights, could only raise legal issues for no material reason." Some states tried to come to a compromise. Alaska lowered its voting age to nineteen; Hawaii only lowered its voting age to twenty.

The Sixties

John F. Kennedy was elected president in November of 1960. Also in 1960, the Twenty-Third Amendment, which gave voting rights in national elections to the residents of Washington, DC, was passed. In 1961, Kennedy proposed to Congress that the vote be extended to eighteen-year-olds in the District of

Columbia. The same year, several bills were introduced that supported the lowering of the voting age in Washington, DC.

Between January 5 and April 13, 1961, seven bills calling for a federally enacted minimum voting age of eighteen were introduced. At least three bills, all suggesting a federally enacted minimum voting age of eighteen, were introduced to Congress between January 1963 and March 1964. How frustrating the process must have been to supporters. From 1925 through 1964, nearly sixty proposals had been introduced to lower the voting age to eighteen.

The Commission on Voter Participation and Registration found that the states should consider a minimum voting age of eighteen. The commission suggested that the main reason for low voter participation in the twenty-one to thirty age group was that by the age of twenty-one, many people have been out of school so long that their interest in public affairs has faded. The commission also made suggestions about additions to school civics programs that would further prepare young people for the vote.

After President Kennedy was assassinated, President Lyndon B. Johnson seemed to favor the notion of states' rights, but also gave some weight to the ballots-for-bullets argument. In his response to the findings of the Commission, he said:

> I am told that it is easier today to buy a destructive weapon, a gun, in a hardware store, than it is to vote. The whole problem that we have in each State in this Union, in each precinct in each State, is to make it easier for people to vote instead of harder. Why should it be difficult for people to vote? It is easier now to register and enlist in the Service in many cases than it is to vote. Why should a man have an

easy path provided for him to go and fight, but a difficult path for him to go and vote? I would say that we should make it as easy for a man to vote as for a man to serve in the Armed Forces. I am hopeful that in the next Presidential election three out of every three eligible voters will vote for their President instead of only two out of every three.

Vietnam and Civil Rights

The 1960s and early 1970s were a time of tremendous change in this country. There were great divides in society created by the Vietnam War, political scandal, and ethnic confrontations brought about by a culture of prejudice. There were protests, marches, and sit-ins. There were murders of civil rights workers who were trying to ensure the rights of African Americans.

Most active in the issues of the day were young people, many of whom still had not been granted the right to vote. And now they really wanted to have their say. As young people protested the war in Vietnam, U.S. forces there were increased to 400,000 in 1965. As young people marched for the rights of African Americans, there were race riots in several major cities in 1966. By 1967, American deaths in Vietnam had reached more than 20,000. By 1968, the question was no longer will young people get the vote, but when?

Young People Prove the Point

Young people were much more politically organized to face the issues of the time than they had been in the past. They formed organizations to defend many causes. A movement called Let Us Vote (LUV) was founded on a college campus in California specifically to fight for a voting age of eighteen. LUV's founder, Dennis Warren, was eventually named to the board of directors of the Youth Franchise Coalition (YFC). The YFC was a coalition of adult and student groups working in support of the lower voting age. Warren made many television appearances, including the *Dating Game* and the *Today Show*, getting the kind of attention the coalition wanted for its cause. Local groups affiliated with the YFC were working in forty states and in Washington, DC.

Since the beginning of World War II, only Georgia and Kentucky had lowered their voting age from twenty-one to eighteen. But the fight for a lower minimum voting age helped to bring about other reforms. Literacy tests were banned and residency requirements were established. Literacy tests were banned as a result of the Supreme Court case *Katzenbach v. Morgan*. The court ruled that imposing a literacy test on Spanish-speaking citizens in New York City violated the rights given them by the Fourteenth Amendment. Standard residency requirements were established by the federal government, something usually left to individual states.

Supreme Court decisions interpreting the Voting Rights Act of 1965 established a type of dual-age system (*Oregon v. Mitchell*). People between the ages of eighteen and twenty-one were allowed to vote in all federal elections, but the states still had the power to set the minimum age for state and local elections. At the time, only three states had already lowered their voting ages to eighteen: Alaska, Georgia, and Kentucky. As a result of the new law, the Census Bureau predicted that about 11.5 million new people would become eligible to vote in the 1972 elections!

In January of 1971, Senator Jennings Randolph again introduced a resolution to amend the Constitution to allow eighteen-year-olds to vote in all elections. He made several points about the dual-age system: "Limiting eighteen-to-twenty-year-olds to voting only for federal officials will place a significant burden on our state and local officials responsible for election practices and procedures—separate voting rolls, and separate ballots in primary and general elections. Clearly, this will be cumbersome and . . . a costly process." He pointed out what a burden this would be to cities already in need of more money.

On March 2, 1971, the House Judiciary Committee approved a constitutional amendment to lower the voting age to eighteen for all elections. On March 23, the House of Representatives approved the amendment. A speedy ratification of the amendment by three-quarters of the states would solve the dual-age dilemma created by the Supreme Court. The 1972 elections were approaching. It took just thirty-six days for twenty-five states (about two-thirds of the number needed) to ratify the amendment, the fastest ratification in history. The amendment became law on June 30, 1971, just 100 days after it was passed by Congress.

In 1972, 48.3 percent of the total eighteen-to-twenty-year-old voting-age population cast their first ballots in the presidential election. In 1996, only 31.2 percent of eligible voters between eighteen and twenty cast their votes for president. In 1998, 13.5 percent of eligible eighteen-to-twenty-year-old voters went to the polls to elect Congresspeople. Given how difficult it was for African Americans, women, young people, and other groups to win their voting rights, it is odd that so many American citizens do not vote.

89

5 The Continuing Struggle over the Right to Vote

After World War II, Americans saw evidence of the changes in their society all around them. The world was a new place. America had proved victorious in the war, but its eyes had been opened to the horror of Hitler and leaders like him. At home, women were voting and holding professional jobs, earning graduate degrees, and helping in the military. African Americans had fought bravely in the war and came home to find opportunities a bit better than they had been. There was a growing, organized push for equality. The National Association for the Advancement of Colored People (NAACP), along with many new political organizations and civic, labor, and religious groups, worked for the cause of equality.

Harry Truman, president from 1945 to 1953, helped to create a climate in which African Americans could improve their status in society. In 1946, he organized a committee, made up of respected black and white Americans, to investigate the quality of civil rights in the country and to make recommendations for their improvement. The report was called "To Secure These Rights." It harshly described how civil rights were being denied to some Americans. The committee called for a program that would "eliminate segregation, based on race, color, creed, or national origin, from American life." Truman also integrated the armed forces in 1949. Truman said that there should be a civil rights program backed by the "full force and power of the federal government" to bring an end to discrimination against minorities.

In the South, segregation policies ruled the day. Black children were not allowed to attend white schools. Water fountains, lunch counters, theaters, and restrooms all had "whites only" or "coloreds only" signs on them. African Americans were expected to sit in the back of public buses. If a white person wanted the seat, the black person was expected to get up.

Many religious institutions and organizations worked to bring an end to this racial hatred. The American Friends Service Committee, the American Missionary Association, the National Council of Churches, the Anti-Defamation League of B'nai B'rith, and many Catholic priests and bishops all performed different services for the cause of equality. The federal government began to chip away at segregation, too. When the Department of the Interior and the City Recreation Board of Washington, DC. were desegregated, African Americans could use all the public parks, playgrounds, and swimming pools within the city. In 1953, the Supreme Court opened all the restaurants in the city to African Americans by upholding a statute from 1872 that required all such places to serve "all well-behaved" people. Newly-elected President Eisenhower said that he hoped this would serve as an example to the rest of the country.

Even after voting rights were secured, segregation policies still existed in the South.

Not everyone was happy about these changes. When in 1956 the Interstate Commerce Commission brought an end to segregation on all interstate trains, buses, and related waiting rooms and depots, some southern states created separate waiting rooms for intrastate black passengers. They followed the letter of the law, but certainly not its spirit.

African Americans and Politics

As many more black people moved to the North and the West, they became politically active. In some cities, such as Chicago, Detroit, and Cleveland, they were a significant force in elections. Even in the South, where the lives of African Americans were so restricted, the number of blacks registering and voting was on the rise. In 1948, 35,000 African Americans voted in the Democratic primary in South Carolina. In the same year, the number of registered black voters in Georgia was more than 150,000. In 1952, 63 percent of eligible black voters in Durham, North Carolina, voted regularly.

African Americans were also being elected. By 1956 there were approximately 40 black representatives in state legislatures, all in the North and West. African Americans were winning local elections, too. Hulan Jack was elected president of the borough of Manhattan, and Rufus E. Clement, president of Atlanta University, was elected to the Atlanta school board in 1953. Thurgood Marshall became solicitor general of the United States in 1965. J. Ernest Wilkins became assistant secretary of labor in

1953, and E. Frederick Morrow was an administrative assistant in the executive offices of the president.

States' Rights

Southern state governments were not anxious to go along with the changes taking place in the rest of the country. In 1956, the governors of South Carolina, Georgia, Mississippi, and Virginia called on all the southern states to declare that the federal government had no authority to prohibit segregation in their states and to "protest in appropriate language, against the encroachment of the central government upon the sovereignty of the several states and their people." In the same year, more than ninety southern members of Congress presented their "Declaration of Constitutional Principles," known as the "Southern Manifesto" in Congress. The document said that the federal government's effort to desegregate the South was a violation of states' rights, and it encouraged states to use "every lawful means" to avoid putting federal policies into action.

Violence was on the rise. In Mississippi, several African American leaders who had urged blacks to vote were murdered. The president of an NAACP chapter was shot when he ignored an order to take his name off the list of registered voters in his town. Citizens in the North and the South began to show anxiety about the ever-increasing racial tensions. Some looked for federal action, but the president and Congress did not step in. The Ku Klux Klan was still going strong, along with other groups that threatened and hurt black people who tried to exercise their civil rights.

Dr. Martin Luther King, Jr.

Born in Atlanta, Georgia, King was a black Baptist minister who led the civil rights movement from the mid-1950s until he was assassinated in Memphis, Tennessee, in 1968. His leadership allowed the movement to be successful in ending segregation. He promoted nonviolent forms of protest such as sit-ins and marches. He served as the president of the Montgomery Improvement Association, a group of black activists in Alabama. In his first speech in this position, he said:

We have no alternative but to protest. For many years we have shown an amazing patience. We have sometimes given our white brothers the feeling that we liked the way we were being treated. But we come here tonight to be saved from that patience that makes us patient with anything less than freedom and justice.

From 1960 to 1965, King organized many protest demonstrations, including the March on Washington in 1963, where he delivered his famous "I Have a Dream" speech. He was arrested and jailed in 1963 for protesting against segregated lunch counters in Birmingham, Alabama. From jail he wrote an explanation of his principles of nonviolence that has come to be known as "The Letter from Birmingham Jail."

You may well ask: 'Why direct action? Why sit-ins, marches, and so forth?' . . . It seeks . . . to dramatize the issue [so] that it can no longer be ignored . . . We know through painful experience that freedom is never voluntarily given by the oppressor; it must be demanded by the oppressed.

King was awarded the Nobel Peace Prize in 1964, and continued his work until his murder in 1968.

95

People participate in a sit-in at the Seattle city hall.

Boycotts, Protests, and Sit-Ins

A boycott is the refusal to buy goods or services or to participate in some activity as a protest. African Americans in Montgomery, Alabama, boycotted the buses to show that they would no longer tolerate sitting in the back. African Americans had decided to use political action to win their rights back.

In 1957, Congress passed the first civil rights bill since 1875. The bill gave the federal government the right to step in where anyone was denied his or her right to vote. The bill also created the United States Commission on Civil Rights. The commission would investigate any accusation that someone had been prevented from voting, and it would evaluate federal laws for their equality of protection.

In 1960, four black college students sat down at a lunch counter in North Carolina for a cup of coffee. Because they were black, they were not served. Because they were determined, they sat there until the store closed. In the same year, white and black young people participated in this sort of protest at white libraries, white beaches, the lobbies of white hotels, and at other lunch counters. They were often arrested. In the *Atlanta Constitution*, black students said, "We do not intend to wait placidly for those rights which are already legally and morally ours to be meted out to us one at a time." Many civil rights leaders emerged in this fight for equal treatment under the law.

There were many demonstrations and protests. President John F. Kennedy worked to expand the civil rights program. He listened to the leaders of the 1963 March on Washington and promised his support for the push for

97

equality. He proposed a bill recommending a new civil rights program. The president was assassinated near the end of 1963 as crimes against African Americans continued.

The Civil Rights Act of 1964

President Lyndon B. Johnson, who took office after Kennedy's death, supported Kennedy's civil rights program. Just a few days after he took office he told Congress that he wanted "the earliest possible passage of the civil rights bill." In the meantime, the Twenty-fourth Amendment to the Constitution was passed in January 1964. The amendment outlawed the poll tax, which had served for a long time as a way to keep blacks from voting in federal elections. The next month, the civil rights bill was passed by the House of Representatives, and in June the bill made it through the Senate. The Civil Rights Act of 1964 is considered by many to be the most far-reaching law in support of racial equality ever enacted by Congress. It gave the attorney general more power to protect American citizens against discrimination and segregation in voting, education, and the use of public facilities. It required the removal of discriminatory policies in federally assisted programs. Those programs could be closed or have the government's financial help taken away if they refused to follow the new law.

There were many people who did not want to enforce the act. In the North, some people resented the protests in their own towns and cities. In the South, there were the usual attempts to keep the old order. The segregationists renamed public places as private clubs to be able to keep blacks out. But the Supreme Court declared that the "public accommodations" section of the act, the part that said that public facilities could not be segregated, was constitutional, and had to be obeyed. The Civil Rights Act did not bring peace to the country. There were race riots and other conflicts that came out of racial tension throughout the Northeast. In the South, the Klan took up the leadership of the movement to defend white supremacy. Hundreds of thousands of African Americans in the South still had a hard time voting, or were kept away from the polls altogether. There was tremendous opposition to voter registration drives among blacks, and many white people who tried to help or support the cause of African Americans also became victims of Klan violence.

The Voting Rights Act of 1965

The failure of the Civil Rights Act of 1964 to restore order and give African Americans the rights they'd actually been given 100 years earlier was a source of disappointment, frustration, and hopelessness to many. Blacks were still unable to participate in the government to which they paid taxes and for which they'd fought wars. They were not able to participate fully in the social and economic life of the country and could not find a healthy environment in which to raise and educate their children.

After the arrest of a young African American charged with reckless driving in the Watts area of Los Angeles, California, an angry crowd gathered. They fought the police. The next day, the crowd grew, the violence increased, and Los Angeles was burning. By the time the

Watts riot was over, there were thirty-four dead, 1,032 injured, and 3,952 arrested. Property damage was estimated at $40 million.

The desegregation process was slow. In the eleven states that had formed the Confederacy during the Civil War, only 6 percent of black children were attending desegregated schools in the 1965-1966 school year. And African Americans were still being kept from participating in elections. In 1965, when Martin Luther King, Jr. announced that the Southern Christian Leadership Conference (SCLC) would begin a voter registration drive in Selma, Alabama, only 335 of the possible 15,115 black voters were registered. The president was being urged to move forward with laws to protect voting rights.

President Johnson sent a bill to Congress that would give the federal government the right to intervene where there were voting problems caused by racial discrimination. It also abolished the use of literacy tests and other methods used to stop blacks from voting. Southern members of Congress argued that the bill violated states' rights. Johnson and the Senate leadership allowed the southerners to have their say but then they put the bill to a vote, and it passed. The bill was tied up in the House of Representatives for a month, where it was found by some to be designed just to punish the South. Eventually, though, it passed. On August 3, 1965, Johnson signed the Voting Rights Act of 1965 into law. He said, "Today is a triumph for freedom as huge as any victory that has ever been won on any battlefield." Johnson promised not to let anything stop the government "until Americans of every race and color and origin in this country have the same rights as all others to share in the progress of democracy."

The Legacy of the Voting Rights Act

Just a few months after the bill became law, thousands of African Americans in the South registered to vote. A few years afterward, there was an increase in the number of black elected officials at all levels of government. Changes were made to the act in 1970, 1975, and 1982. In 1975, amendments were made to the act to protect the voting rights of non-English-speaking citizens. In 1982, the act was amended so that, instead of having to prove that someone had the intention of discriminating against the voter, it simply had to be shown that the person's actions had resulted in discrimination against the voter.

Now that the federal government was able to control the polling policies of each state, African Americans could finally participate in the government as citizens of the United States. In 1997, there were 617 black elected officials at the federal and state levels, and 5,052 in city and county positions. Women worked very hard, too, to win the right to vote and hold office. In 1998, there were eighty-two women holding state offices. The right to vote gives Americans the power to stop injustice by electing leaders whose policies protect us and preserve our democracy. It's hard to imagine why anyone would not vote if they could.

Preamble to the Constitution

We the People of the United States, in order to form a more perfect Union, establish Justice, insure domestic Tranquility, provide for the common defence, promote the general Welfare, and secure the Blessings of Liberty to ourselves and our Posterity, do ordain and establish this Constitution for the United States of America.

On September 25, 1789, Congress transmitted to the state legislatures twelve proposed amendments, two of which, having to do with congressional representation and congressional pay, were not adopted. The remaining ten amendments became the Bill of Rights.

The Bill of Rights

Amendment I
Congress shall make no law respecting an establishment of religion, or prohibiting the free exercise thereof; or abridging the freedom of speech, or of the press; or the right of the people peaceably to assemble, and to petition the Government for a redress of grievances.

Amendment II
A well regulated Militia, being necessary to the security of a free State, the right of the people to keep and bear Arms, shall not be infringed.

Amendment III
No Soldier shall, in time of peace be quartered in any house, without the consent of the Owner, nor in time of war, but in a manner to be prescribed by law.

Amendment IV
The right of the people to be secure in their persons, houses, papers, and effects, against unreasonable searches and seizures, shall not be violated, and no Warrants shall issue, but upon probable cause, supported by Oath or affirmation, and particularly describing the place to be searched, and the persons or things to be seized.

Amendment V

No person shall be held to answer for a capital, or otherwise infamous crime, unless on a presentment or indictment of a Grand Jury, except in cases arising in the land or naval forces, or in the Militia, when in actual service in time of War or public danger; nor shall any person be subject for the same offence to be twice put in jeopardy of life or limb; nor shall be compelled in any criminal case to be a witness against himself, nor be deprived of life, liberty, or property, without due process of law; nor shall private property be taken for public use, without just compensation.

Amendment VI

In all criminal prosecutions, the accused shall enjoy the right to a speedy and public trial, by an impartial jury of the State and district wherein the crime shall have been committed, which district shall have been previously ascertained by law, and to be informed of the nature and cause of the accusation; to be confronted with the witnesses against him; to have compulsory process for obtaining witnesses in his favor, and to have the Assistance of Counsel for his defence.

Amendment VII

In Suits at common law, where the value in controversy shall exceed twenty dollars, the right of trial by jury shall be preserved, and no fact tried by a jury, shall be otherwise re-examined in any Court of the United States, than according to the rules of the common law.

Amendment VIII

Excessive bail shall not be required, nor excessive fines imposed, nor cruel and unusual punishments inflicted.

Amendment IX

The enumeration in the Constitution, of certain rights, shall not be construed to deny or disparage others retained by the people.

Amendment X

The powers not delegated to the United States by the Constitution, nor prohibited by it to the States, are reserved to the States respectively, or to the people.

Glossary

abolition   The movement to make slavery illegal.

abridge   To cut short; to limit.

activist   A person who participates in political marches, social protests, and other activities for a cause.

amendment   A change that is made to a law or legal document.

Congress   The branch of the United States government that makes laws. It is made up of the Senate and the House of Representatives.

constitution   A document that establishes the fundamental laws of a state or country.

delegate   Someone who represents other people.

enfranchise   The act of giving someone the right to vote.

federal   Pertaining to the national government.

feminist   Someone who believes that women should have the same rights and the same opportunities as men.

House of Representatives   One of the houses of Congress that makes laws. The number of members for each state is based on the state's population. Members have two-year terms.

integration   The practice of making facilities open to people of all races.

legislation   Laws that have been proposed or passed.

ratify   To approve officially.

Senate   One of the houses of Congress that makes laws. Each state has two senators, who are elected every six years.

states' rights   The belief that state governments have greater authority than the federal government on certain issues.

suffrage   The right to vote.

suffragette   A name sometimes given to women who fought for women's suffrage.

Supreme Court   The highest and most powerful court in the United States. It can declare laws unconstitutional.

veto   To stop a bill from becoming a law.

For More Information

In the United States

American Civil Liberties Union (ACLU)
125 Broad Street, 18th floor
New York, NY 10004
(212) 344-3005
Web site: http://www.aclu.org

Kids Voting USA
398 South Mill Avenue, Suite 304
Tempe, AZ 85281
(480) 921-3727
e-mail: kidsvotingusa@kidsvotingusa.org
Web site: http://kidsvotingusa.org

Rock the Vote
10635 Santa Monica Boulevard, Box 22
Los Angeles, CA 90025

(310) 234-0665
e-mail: mail@rockthevote.org
Web site: http://www.rockthevote.org

Young Politicians of America
P.O. Box 5286
Walnut Creek, CA 94596-1286
e-mail: shelton@ypa.org
Web site: http://www.ypa.org

In Canada

Forum for Young Canadians
P.O. Box 2103, Station D
Ottawa, ON K1P 5W3
(613) 233-4086
e-mail: forum@forum.ca
Web site: http://www.forum.ca

Web Sites

Canadian Elections on the Internet
http://www.library.ubc.ca/poli/cpweb.html

Nelson Political Science
http://polisci.nelson.com/elections.html

For Further Reading

Banfield, Susan. *The Fifteenth Amendment: African-American Men's Right to Vote*. Springfield, NJ: Enslow Publishers, 1998.

Bartlett, John W. (ed.) *The Future Is Ours: A Handbook for Student Activists in the 21st Century*. New York: H. Holt and Co., 1996.

Dash, Joan. *We Shall Not Be Moved: The Women's Factory Strike of 1909*. New York: Scholastic, 1998.

Dubois, Ellen Carol. *Feminism and Suffrage: The Emergence of an Independent Women's Movement, 1848–1869*. Ithaca, NY: Cornell University Press, 1999.

Kendall, Martha E. *Susan B. Anthony: Voice for Women's Voting Rights*. Springfield, NJ: Enslow, 1997.

Keyssar, Alexander. *The Right to Vote: The Contested History of Democracy in the United States*. New York: Basic Books, 2000.

Lawson, Steven F. *Black Ballots: Voting Rights in the South, 1944–1969*. Lanham, MD: Lexington Books, 1999.

Lusane, Clarence. *No Easy Victories: Black Americans and the Vote.* New York: Franklin Watts, 1996.

Miles, Harvey. *Women's Voting Rights.* Danbury, CT: Children's Press, 1998.

Monroe, Judy. *The Nineteenth Amendment: Women's Right to Vote.* Springfield, NJ: Enslow Publishers, 1998.

Scher, Linda. *The Vote: Making Your Voice Heard.* Austin, TX: Raintree Steck-Vaughn, 1996.

Sobel, Syl. *How the U.S. Government Works.* Hauppauge, NY: Barron's, 1999.

Index

Photo Credits
Cover image: The Constitution of the United States of America; p.8 © Kevin Fleming/Corbis; p.15, 43, 67, 81 © Corbis; p.19, 27, 31, 34, 47, 61, 69, 92 © Archive Photos; p. 23 © American Stock/Archive Photos; p.77 © Leif Skoogfors/Corbis, p. 95 © Flip Schulke/Corbis; p. 96 © Seattle Post–Intelligencer Collection; Museum of History & Industry.

Series Design and Layout
Danielle Goldblatt